£5

D0319940

TRIES!

TRIES!

GERALD DAVIES

Edited by
DAVID PARRY-JONES

HARRAP LONDON

First published in Great Britain 1984
by HARRAP LIMITED
19-23 Ludgate Hill, London EC4M 7PD

© *Gerald Davies* 1984

All rights reserved. No part of this
publication may be reproduced in any
form or by any means without the prior
permission of Harrap Limited.

ISBN 0 245-54203-5

Designed by Michael R. Carter

Printed and bound in Great Britain
by R. J. Acford, Chichester.

CONTENTS

ACKNOWLEDGMENTS

We are indebted to all the players, past and present, who found the
time to contribute to this volume. We thank them all, and are
extremely grateful for their response.
They were asked to nominate a favourite try which they
themselves scored or took part in, and to give the reason for their
choice. They were also asked if they might care to select a favourite
try witnessed. In this second case there was one stipulation: they
were not to include the famous Barbarian try scored against New
Zealand in 1973. Primarily for the sake of variety, they were asked
to exclude the opening score of that match. Rightly or wrongly, we
believed that that try is so firmly embedded in the legends of
Rugby football that it inspires universal admiration and affection.
We felt that the immediate, almost involuntary, response of the
majority of people to the question would be to nominate that great
try. A period of further reflection might even still produce the
same answer. Such is its magic.
We also said that a 'witnessed try' meant that they had to have
been present at the ground to see it. We feared that matches have
been replayed so often on television, that memory might play tricks
on so many that they might have come to believe that they were
actually there for instance to see Phil Bennett, J.P.R. Williams,
John Pullin, John Dawes, Tom David, Derek Quinnell run
desperately and majestically out of defence, and to savour the thrill
(regardless of parochial loyalties) of Gareth Edwards's dramatic
and exultant dive for the line.

We wish to thank the following sources for permission to
reproduce the photographs:

BBC Television Wales, pages 112, 113, 114, 115, 116

Colorsport, pages 1, 2, 7, 9, 11, 14, 16, 18, 19, 20, 23, 24, 25, 26, 28,
30, 31, 36, 37, 38, 46, 47, 50, 53, 54, 58, 67, 69, 71, 76, 77, 80, 85,
89, 93, 94, 95, 97, 99, 100, 101, 103, 104

Press Association, pages ix, 4, 5, 33, 44, 61

Rugby World, page 3

Sports & General Press Agency, page 62

The Times, page 43

PREFACE

By Gerald Davies

'Do you remember . . . ?' And with those three alluring words the evocation begins. With fresh eyes in a quiet room or in a men's four-ale bar, you see the drama unfold again, as if on some grainy sepia-faded film. The crowning glory of THE TRY that once held the breath, that drew the applause and deserved the laurel wreath.

Tries, the constant hope and anxious anticipation of which are what shifts and lifts a drifting, seemingly aimless flux of a match away from the thick consistency of that Wall Game they play at Eton to an altogether different realm of excitement and drama, and which makes people fit for poetry. Penalties, more prosaically, may still win the day, and reliable kickers, monotonously practical, prove a more indispensable ingredient on any national selector's shopping-list. In moments of reflection, however, as well as the stirring time of action, more precious by far are those men who by wit and invention, will and persistence, power and strength, cross the opposing line for the touch-down. That is always a spectacular moment. Whether the passage of play flows with a swift and easy motion, or is full of incoherent strokes, tries bring it all to an absolute pause; the very action is a devastating full-stop. Rugby without them — and people somehow managed in the early days — would hardly exist.

It is, after all, a curious egg of a game which allows, uniquely for a major sport, four different methods of accumulating points. Those who are new to the game are often bewildered by it; those steeped in its intricate ways love to spend time arguing about the merits of this or that decision. That the tally of points for the scoring chances should also differ no doubt contributes to the game's rich pattern or quite simply adds to the general confusion. In other sports there is a singular uniformity: a goal is a goal in football, a point is a point in badminton or squash. And the objective in golf is simply to get the ball into the hole. Each is clearly defined.

More curious still, and to add to the heart-rending frustration, most of the points in any one game accrue from some mysterious technical transgression which the referee sees and no-one else does. Or if the observer does, then he is just as likely to disagree. No other sport relies so grossly on such infringements for a team to gain superiority, and less on its skills and tactical nous to gain points advantage. There is no honour in the inevitable progress of such a contrivance.

After all is said and done tries are the vital essence of an earthy contest of primitive force and strength. In brief, shining moments with a perverse mixture of good fortune and refined artistry, giftedness and surprising enterprise, or power and collective will, not forgetting a little shuffle and blunder now and then, the defence of the best is found wanting, and the white line is magically crossed. Against the backdrop of much heaving and pushing, tries provide moments of clarity and sharpness. However they are achieved, whatever the method, they bring to fruition a team's or an individual player's efforts. Our hopes, once seen to be quickly fading in a penalty-strewn match, are fulfilled, and our languishing faith returns and feeds our boyish hearts. The best-laid plans, we may be convinced, do not after all come to nought.

'Enough of these penalties' the cry perennially goes up. 'Let's have more tries!' To which the sceptic might answer that a surfeit may only serve to sicken and it is the rarity value that matters. Are we not also so conditioned, for the want of a child's sense of wonder, to cry out that too many tries make it less of a 'proper' game? Others, so misguided, prefer to highlight the weakness in defence and not acknowledge the brilliance of attack. Whatever is elusive and creative may be considered disparagingly as pretty and clever and not worth the candle. The bruising play is seen as the reality and the delicate touch as so much veneer. It is an idea which deceives only ultimately to flatter.

The try is the quickening life of the game. It is what stimulates the intellect and animates the emotions. A penalty is of interest in a dry, mathematical sense: it keeps the scoreboards ticking over. A try adds to an heroic kind of beauty and creates a legend. It is what endures.

The heart still beats apprehensively; that somehow along the line the try is only an inch away from failure. Nightly — almost — the flicker of fear returns at the recognition of a run which, but for the timely arch of the back, an intake of breath, a momentary combination of nerve and muscle and a final exultant lunge, would not have brought success. An instant, elusive vision that anything just might be possible. And it is over. One efficient moment of spontaneity, or premeditation even, never to be repeated quite like that again.

Richard Sharp arched his back and felt fingers run down his spine and scored against Scotland; Andy Hancock teetered on the touch-line to the anguish of the Scots in the Twickenham crowd; Ian Kirkpatrick staved off tackles to left and right of him in Christchurch in 1971; and the ball for J. J. Williams stood up on its

viii

point in the raging heat of South Africa; 'go for it,' were the three words of his childhood mentor Bill Samuel that reverberated through Gareth Edwards's mind as his finger-nails got there ahead of a desperate Scottish defence. An inch the other way — and the whole courageous enterprise would have failed.

Gerald Davies in typical try-scoring action for Wales against Ireland in 1971.

These are moments of glory which come to few. John Pullin in his answer imagined such a try he might like to have scored by running out of defence but had to content himself with charging over from a ruck close to the South African line. More plaintively Jeff Young, the Welsh hooker, though he apologized for not nominating a try for this volume, did say that he had crossed the line twice. Once during an inspection of the pitch at Twickenham, and once when he was carried off on a stretcher in Pretoria!

Not all front-row forwards are so out of luck. Graham Price of Wales, in his first International, ran the length of Parc des Princes to score an unforgettable try in the dying moments. For Mike Roberts, again for Wales, 'a six inch-dash for the line' was all it took but was equally memorable for him in his last International match. For both of them, tries were a rare joy.

For my part, with just a little bit of luck and the company of good men, I managed to score twenty for Wales. Although not all of them hold a treasured place — indeed I would have to be reminded of a few — some of course are special, as is broadly true of the ones I scored for the British Lions. Favourite tries can be chosen for a variety of reasons: they may be important in the context of winning a particular match, or because of the speed or the skill involved; or perhaps because of the level of difficulty, or of the grand occasions on which they were scored.

In my own case it is in terms of pure affection and the warmth of feeling they still inspire that I would choose my four tries against Pontypool one bleak midwinter afternoon in the quarter-final of the 1978 Schweppes Cup competition. The myth has grown that I touched the ball only on those four occasions, and I'm not going to argue with that, although I would like to think that I did contribute something else to my team's effort. To all intents and purposes the ominous power and relentless drive of the Pontypool pack on that day should have destroyed Cardiff by half-time. But courage, spirit and determination — call it what you will — never allowed us to cave in. And when I think of the four tries I think of the whole team battling against the odds, and the pride I felt as captain.

It is with a sense of apology to all those I knew so well in the seventies, and the great tries I saw them score, that my choice of favourite witnessed try comes from outside that decade. I cannot distance myself sufficiently from them; I was too much part of the swelling scene. I was, you might say, too close to the reality: too close to the sweat and the spit. Through rose-coloured glasses I think of the schoolboy who stood disbelievingly on the tanner bank in Stradey one floodlit midweek game and saw D. Ken Jones dance his way through the whole Irish Wolfhounds team — or so it seemed — to dive majestically, as he did in South Africa in the First Test of 1962, under the posts. A club game it might have been, but his try encapsulated what I wanted Rugby to be.

That all greatness is gone and that only the worst remains is deservedly contradicted in these pages. There is a line of great tries stretching from the twenties to the present day. That memorable tries have been, and still are, scored finds ample testimony here. They do not fade quietly away; they remain vivid. In recollection they are precious.

> For in the auditorium the echoes linger
> And never completely die away.
> Fame is the far-off and never-dying legend
> Of the artist's pride . . .

So wrote Idris Davies in *The Retired Actor*. It is the same for the Rugby player. He is not an old romantic ruin. For in a kindly, reflective mood he will mellow once more in this year's September sun. At the start of another season he will smell the freshly-mown grass and wintergreen, and hear the clatter of studs and the shouts from the terraces. And when dropped goals look deceptively easy, yet eminently forgettable; when penalties are given with monotonous regularity and contrive to frustrate, the cry will go up, 'Let's have a try, then!' And if when it comes it is good, that is the memory that will be taken home and cherished.

Robert Ackerman

(Newport, London Welsh, Wales & British Isles)
16 caps for Wales (1980-84), 2 Tests for British
Isles (1983) as a centre.
Now lives in Newport.

MOST MEMORABLE TRY SCORED
Ireland (9) v Wales (18), Dublin, 4.2.1984

My second half-try originated at a line-out near
half-way on an Irish throw. Normally our
back-line would have been lying shallow to
pressure opponents on their expected possession. But before this game the Welsh coach, John
Bevan, had predicted that we would win plenty
of line-out ball even when the throw was against
our forwards, and had urged the backs to lie
deep away from our defensive area. So it proved
on this occasion, with the result that by the time
the ball reached me I was up to full speed.

Next I was able to brush my way past the Irish
cover defence, but still had forty odd metres to
go, with the full-back to beat. Here it was that
Hugo McNeill bought a dummy I threw in the
direction of 'Ikey' Stephens, and the way to the
line was clear.

This was my first try for Wales, and certainly
worth waiting fourteen games for!

MOST MEMORABLE TRY WITNESSED
New Zealand (15) v British Isles (8), Dunedin, 2.7.1983

On a waterlogged pitch the Lions won a line-out
in the All Blacks' 22. Roy Laidlaw, Ollie Campbell, Michael Kiernan and John Rutherford all
handled smoothly, the last-named missing out
full-back Gwyn Evans and serving Roger Baird
on the left wing. Baird beat his opposite number
on the outside before flipping the ball to the
supporting Evans who, despite being tackled
four metres short of the line, managed to send a
scoring pass back inside to Rutherford.

I choose this try because the Lions' handling
was so very good in the awful playing conditions. Also, to break down such a well-
organized defence as that of the All Blacks from
a set-piece was very gratifying.

Moments from the move which led to a glorious try for the British Lions in the 1983 Dunedin Test. Roger Baird seems to have beaten his man (previous page), but is nevertheless nailed by Stu Wilson (top). However, he gets the ball away to Gwyn Evans, who put John Rutherford in for a try, much to the latter's clench-fisted delight (bottom).

Rodger Arneil

(Edinburgh Academicals, Leicester, Northampton, Scotland & British Isles)
22 caps for Scotland (1968-73), 4 Tests for British Isles (1968) as a flanker.
Now lives near Oxford.

Alan Ashcroft

(Waterloo, England & British Isles)
16 caps for England (1956-59), 2 tests for British Isles (1959) as a back-row forward.
Now lives near Ormskirk, Lancashire.

MOST MEMORABLE TRY SCORED
St Mary's School, Melrose, v Merchiston School, autumn 1956

A nostalgic recall from schooldays when I had already become an apprentice flanker. My try began on our own line from where I seem to remember running through fourteen opponents to score at the other end of the pitch. I can still 'feel' that try today, together with the excitement of swerving and side-stepping past defenders.

MOST MEMORABLE TRY WITNESSED
Scotland (18) v Wales (19), Murrayfield, 6.2.1971

I choose the try by Gerald Davies in this match not necessarily for the speed which the Welsh wing showed in beating our full-back, Ian Smith, but because the score was achieved with Wales under great pressure. The minutes were slipping away with Scotland 18-14 up, and it showed marvellous ability for the visitors to keep plugging away and finally produce the try which, converted by John Taylor, won an exciting game.

MOST MEMORABLE TRY SCORED
Combined Transvaal (18) v Barbarians (16), Johannesburg, 24.5.1958

The Barbarians' final try (in a spectacular game which contained four by each side) swept the whole length of the field. It started with Cliff Morgan giving Tony O'Reilly a speculative pass close to our line, whereupon the tall Irishman used his great stride and swerve to beat both opposing centres. Malcolm Thomas on the wing stayed with him to continue the move, and I managed to finish it off by diving over the top of four would-be tacklers to score in a horizontal position.

MOST MEMORABLE TRY WITNESSED
New Zealand (6) v British Isles (9), Auckland, 19.9.1959

Bev Risman's try was the vital score in beating the All Blacks. It was a superb solo try, characterized by superb side-stepping down the blind side.

Alan Ashcroft is horizontal as he dives over for the Barbarians' fourth try against Combined Transvaal in May 1958. It was the culmination of a move that travelled the length of the field.

Roger Baird

(Kelso, Scotland & British Isles)
16 caps for Scotland (1981-84), 4 Tests for British
Isles (1983) as a wing.
Now lives in Edinburgh.

*Andy Irvine is injured, but not for long, after scoring one of his
two tries in a great Scottish revival against the French in 1980.*

MOST MEMORABLE PARTICIPATION IN TRY
Wales (18) v Scotland (34), Cardiff, 20.3.1982

Wales were 3-0 up and attacking through a ball
hoisted into the Scottish 22. Having covered
across, I found myself behind the catcher, Bill
Cuthbertson, and remember being annoyed
that he kicked instead of passing back to me.
The kick went down the throat of Clive Rees
who immediately went right at speed to link
with Gareth Davies and give our opponents a
two-man overlap.

I was meanwhile desperately trying to get
back to the left wing when, to my surprise,
Davies chipped the ball over the top; the ball
bounced once and came straight up into my
arms. I was at full tilt, so was Wales's Rob
Ackerman who could not change direction to
intercept me, and before I knew it I was round
him — and still in play. Now there seemed to be
all the room in the world. I drew Welsh
full-back Gwyn Evans and passed to Iain Paxton
who had come from nowhere to support on the
inside. Lengthening his stride he reached the
Welsh 22 where, despite being brilliantly tackled
by Clive Rees, he still managed to pass to Alan
Tomes who must have covered three-quarters
of the pitch to be in support. On being tackled
by Gareth Davies he slipped the ball to the
ever-present Jim Calder who went over the line
with Ray Gravell holding onto him.

I choose this try because I think it had a little
bit of everything — counter-attack, hard running and support. Above all, it caught people's
imagination and seemed to set the game alight.
From a Scottish point of view, that is!

MOST MEMORABLE TRY WITNESSED
Scotland (22) v France (14), Murrayfield, 16.2.1980

From a good Scottish scrum deep inside their
half the ball was moved to Bruce Hay. Whistling
up inside him Andy Irvine took his pass and
jinked off the left foot inside Bustaffa without

losing any pace. As the French cover closed him
down he flipped inside to David Johnston. Hay,
again, and John Rutherford also handled before Andy popped up again to score a remarkable try in the left-hand corner. He also converted from the touch-line, starting off an
incredible revival by Scotland who came from
nowhere to win the game with 18 points in ten
minutes.

What was more remarkable, Andy had suffered a nightmarish first half, missing six
penalties including one in front of the posts. His
two tries and 16 points in all in the second half
seemed to me to make up for it!

Bill Beaumont

(Fylde, England & British Isles)
34 caps for England (1975-82), 7 Tests for British Isles (1977-80 as a lock-forward.
Now lives in Preston, Lancashire.

MOST MEMORABLE PARTICIPATION IN TRY
England (23) v Scotland (17), Twickenham, 21.2.1981

Following a line-out Clive Woodward received the ball in midfield on a scissors move, cut back towards the forwards and beat five or six Scottish defenders on his way to the line. It was a fine piece of individual running.

I choose this score because, for just about the first time in my international career, a try came from possession which I had secured at a line-out.

MOST MEMORABLE TRY WITNESSED
Wales (3) v New Zealand (23), Cardiff, 1.11.1980

This try was scored by Graham Mourie, the All Blacks' skipper. Wales had come upfield as far as the New Zealand ten-metre line. Here the ball was pinched by the visitors' back row, who put under way a counter-attack spearheaded by Bruce Robertson. The ball was interpassed half a dozen times and ended up with Mourie who crossed at the corner.

I choose this try because it showed what can be achieved by a side counter-attacking from a defensive position with all its players running in support.

Clive Woodward scores for England against Scotland in 1981 after working a scissors move.

Dewi Bebb

(Carmarthen TC, Swansea, Wales & British Isles)
34 caps for Wales (1959-67), 8 Tests for British
Isles (1962-66) as a wing.
Now lives in Pontyclun, Mid Glamorgan.

MOST MEMORABLE TRY SCORED
France (20) v Wales (14), Paris, 2.4.1967

My try came at a crucial moment. Well into the
second half the score stood at 9-9 with France
pounding away near our line. Then a move on
their right broke down, the ball ran loose and the
instinctive thing for me was to start half hacking,
half dribbling it towards the French line some 70
yards away. For what seemed an eternity I raced
onwards with a series of hacks, constantly aware
of pursuing Frenchmen and with all sorts of
thoughts running through my mind: how close
were the defenders behind me? Should I slow
down to pick the ball up? Will it bounce
favourably into my grasp? Will an unkind
bounce make it run away?

Fortunately I managed to steer the ball well
enough to tap it over the opponents' line and
drop on it exhausted, possibly more through the
mental than the physical exertion of the effort.

The conversion by Terry Price put us ahead
14-9, but we were not to be the first Welsh team
to win in Paris for ten years, the French hitting
back with 11 more points.

Of the tries I scored for Wales this seems to be
the one best remembered by supporters. It was
not a classic try, but the excitement of the
moment and the uncertainty of what was going
to happen lingers in the memory. It also reflects
my philosophical approach to Rugby in the
sixties as a wing three-quarter: if the ball did not
come to hand, the wing had to search for it and
make the most of any scrap of possession coming
his way. Chase until one dropped, if need be!

MOST MEMORABLE TRY WITNESSED
South Africa (3) v British Isles (3), Johannesburg, 23.6.1962

Imagine a packed Ellis Park, the crowd still
buzzing with excitement after witnessing a
spectacular John Gainsford try, but also
apprehensive that the Springboks were ahead by
only 3-0.

With some 15 minutes left of what had been a
fierce encounter between two evenly matched
teams Mannetjies Roux broke towards the right
and kicked ahead. The Lions' full-back John
Willcox fielded the ball, side-stepped the
onrushing Roux, and linked with flanker Budge
Rogers outside whom Ken Jones came sweeping
to take a pass. Off he went at full throttle, leaving
the Springbok wing Ormonde Thomas
floundering with a classic outside swerve.

There were still some 70 yards between him
and the South African line and from my position
as a touch-judge (each team provided a touch-
judge in those days, even in a Test match) it
seemed that Ken would never get there. The last
defender was the immaculate Lionel Wilson
whom Ken left grasping at thin air with a
superbly timed side-step. His try gave the Lions a
share of the spoils.

The South African crowd was generous in its
applause. It had witnessed one of the best tries
ever scored at Ellis Park — by a back who was also
at his best. In ten seconds he demonstrated most
of the requirements for a centre three-quarter:
sheer pace, the outside swerve, beautifully
balanced running, the side-step at speed and
gritty determination.

Ian Beer
(Harlequins & England)
2 caps for England (1955) as a flanker.
Now lives in Harrow.

Phil Bennett
(Llanelli, Wales & British Isles)
29 caps for Wales (1969-78), 8 Tests for British Isles (1974-78), mainly as a stand-off half.
Now lives in Llanelli, Dyfed.

MOST MEMORABLE TRY SCORED
England (9) v Scotland (6), Twickenham, 19.3.1955

From a set piece on the England left (we were playing towards the North Stand) and just outside Scotland's 25 the ball was sent in a very orthodox way along the line to our right wing Frank Sykes. When held he passed inside to myself, backing up from the blind-side flanker position, and I scored at the corner.

I choose the try because it was the only one I scored in a big match — and because it was the winning try in the 1955 Calcutta Cup match.

Phil Bennett – scorer of many marvellous tries. His personal favourite is the one he scored against the Springboks for the British Lions at Pretoria in June 1974.

MOST MEMORABLE TRY SCORED
South Africa (9) v British Isles (28), Pretoria, 22.6.1974

The Springboks were attacking near the half-way line when one of our back-row men tackled Jan Ellis and set up a maul. Flanker Fergus Slattery emerged with the ball, heading left towards the narrow, touch-line side. We executed a scissors move which put me into the open. I was chased by my opposite number Gerald Bosch, but managed to outpace him and was left with the task of beating the full-back Ian McCallum. Feinting to go on the outside, at the last second I came off my right foot to side-step him and go over unopposed.

The try was important to me because our victory over South Africa in the first Test at Cape Town took place at sea level and in deep mud, prompting most South African critics to predict that when we reached Pretoria's altitude and firm grounds the Lions would struggle. It gave me great satisfaction to show them that we were capable of scoring tries in any conditions.

MOST MEMORABLE TRY WITNESSED
Llanelli (9) v South Africa (10), Llanelli, 20.1.1970

In wet, muddy conditions Llanelli moved the ball from just ouside their 25, Clive John, Selwyn Williams and others combining to send Roy Mathias clear. Tackled at half-way the wing nevertheless managed to keep the ball alive with an inside pass to forwards who were in close support and able to resupply Selwyn Williams. The scrum-half worked the narrow side and again there was a storming run by Mathias who was finally cut off by the South African cover.

But the attack was far from dead. Mathias's inside pass sent centre John Thomas clear inside the Springboks' 25 where it took a solid tackle from full-back H. O. de Villiers to halt him a few yards short of the line. Yet again the Scarlets' forwards got to the breakdown, kept the ball alive and transferred it to the backs. Some superb handling ended with full-back Hamilton Jones sending right-wing Alan Richards in at the corner for a truly magnificent try.

I have two main reasons for picking this try. When Llanelli scored it the game was well into the second half, by which time the pitch was heavy and the ball slippery. It was remarkable to see the accurate handling with which forwards and backs kept play alive, not to mention the stamina needed to keep the move going.

Secondly, when you consider that the average age of the Llanelli team was around 21 (lock-forward Delme Thomas and I sat the game out in the stand since we were due to play for Wales on the following Saturday), it was a wonderful performance to limit a near full-strength South African touring side to a one-point win. Dawie de Villiers, Frik du Preez, Jan Ellis, Piet Greyling, Piet Visagie, Mof Myburgh and H. O. de Villiers played at Stradey that day.

John C. Bevan
Cardiff, Wales & British Isles)
10 caps for Wales (1971-73), 1 Test for British Isles (1971) as a wing.
Now lives in Blackpool.

MOST MEMORABLE TRY SCORED
Wales (20) v France (6), Cardiff, 25.3.1972

In a close game the ball was moved along the line, reaching me on the left wing near the half-way line. Although France's wing Duprat had me covered, he made a mistake in the timing of his tackle which allowed me to hand him off and run on the outside away from the cover. Confronted by the full-back, Villepreux, I chose the right option by kicking over his head and winning the race for the touchdown.

Wales needed to win this match to remain unbeaten for two seasons. My try gave me particular satisfaction because although I had scored solo tries for the Lions in New Zealand, this was my first for my country on Welsh soil.

MOST MEMORABLE TRY WITNESSED
Scotland (9) v Wales (18), Murrayfield, 19.3.1977

I enjoyed watching Phil Bennett's try because it smacked more of the Barbarians than a team engaged in a dour Home International.

The Scots were attacking hard on the visitors' 25 when the ball went loose. Instead of using a safe option Wales decided to run the ball and counter-attacked through Gerald Davies. The flair of individuals and the intensive support play that followed was a joy to see, and any one of three men could have scored in the end.

The willingness of forwards and backs to run the ball from a dangerous situation made this try very special. All present — except possibly the Scottish XV — appreciated what they had seen.

(opposite)
John Bevan touches down for his first try for Wales in front of his home fans; Pierre Villepreux trails desperately behind him.

R. W. ('Ronnie') Boon

(Cardiff & Wales)
12 caps for Wales (1930-33) as a wing.
Now lives in Barry, South Glamorgan.

MOST MEMORABLE TRY SCORED
Cardiff (5) v South Africa (13), Cardiff, 21.11.1931

This try is the one I scored for Cardiff. My opposing wing was Maurice Zimmerman of Transvaal, and it was the length of pass I received from Graham Jones which enabled me to round him and run for the line. The crossfield cover was not able to reach me and I was faced finally with beating Brand, South Africa's full-back. I felt confident of scoring for two reasons: first, he was too close to the line and my momentum was bound to knock him backwards and, second, I had 'pointed' him — that is, made him hesitate with the suggestion of an inside swerve.

I choose this try because it involved speed, determination, an awareness of the covering defence, and a climactic conclusion with the wing crossing the line near the corner flag.

MOST MEMORABLE TRY WITNESSED
Wales (8) v Scotland (11), Cardiff, 3.2.1923

The try I have in my memory is that scored by A. L. Gracie, Scotland's captain. His side needed to score to win, and the game had reached its final minutes. Then Gracie received a pass just outside the Welsh 25, ran diagonally for the gap between Arthur Cornish, the Welsh centre, and his wing 'Codger' Johnson, got between them, reached the corner and finally ran round to put the ball down between the posts and seal Scotland's first win at Cardiff Arms Park since 1890.

At no-side the crowd surged onto the field to lift Gracie onto their shoulders and carry him to the dressing rooms!

Onllwyn Brace

(Oxford University, Llanelli & Wales)
9 caps for Wales (1956-61) as a scrum-half.
Now lives in Cowbridge, South Glamorgan.

MOST MEMORABLE PARTICIPATION IN TRY
Wales (9) v Scotland (3), Cardiff, 4.2.1956

This was the infamous 'brazier match' when gangs of fire-tenders worked through the night to make a bone-hard pitch playable. Even so, the surface was semi-frozen and treacherous, and the game ought not to have taken place.

However, at a scrum 15 yards from the Scottish line and 20 yards from the north touch-line I pre-arranged with my stand-off half Cliff Morgan an 'Oxford reverse'. The pack did their job and won good quick ball. I ran flat, flipped a reverse pass to Cliff, who took it at speed and sprinted in unopposed at the city end for the try which made our victory secure.

It may sound simple, but to have planned and executed such a move successfully against an international back row comprising Jim Greenwood, Ian MacGregor and Adam Robson was very satisfying, especially as critics had been warning that the pairing of two individually inclined half-backs like Morgan and Brace would never work. To contrive a score close to the scrum on a treacherous surface was also very pleasing.

For me personally it was gratifying that the Oxford 'switch tactics' of 1955 could be translated into the international arena and were not the sole prerogative of privileged undergraduates who had worked on such moves for days and months on end. In fact, the sole run-out I had with Cliff Morgan was on the Friday before the international — we tried out the move once only, and repeated it to great effect the following afternoon!

MOST MEMORABLE TRY WITNESSED
Llanelli (9) v South Africa (10), Stradey Park, 20.1.1970

The try Llanelli scored after 15 minutes of the second half will be talked about for generations. It involved the whole Llanelli team, some men more than once. A check on the telerecording of the game confirms that the ball passed through 26 pairs of hands, a remarkable feat in its own right. The only boot which touched the ball in three minutes was the one that secured the ball at a ruck — otherwise it was hands all the way and a final dive over the line by wing Alun Richards.

Applauded by the crowd for fully two minutes, this was as good a team try as could be imagined — against the Springbok Test XV.

Peter Brown
(West of Scotland, Gala & Scotland)
27 caps for Scotland (1964-73) as lock and number eight.
Now lives at Melrose, Borders.

MOST MEMORABLE PARTICIPATION IN TRY
England (15) v Scotland (16), Twickenham, 20.3.1971

Chris Rea's 79th-minute try — and my conversion — is remembered by most Scots for securing our first win at Twickenham since 1939. To me it meant much more.

In January 1971, having been made captain of Scotland, I introduced to the team my ideas about a more adventurous, confident approach. We performed well in Paris, leading until a cruel injury blow lost us the match. Next we played to my new plan in the well-remembered 19-18 defeat by Wales, and there followed a disappointing bad-weather mauling by Ireland, also at home. Three games — three losses! Twickenham, with its long hoodoo of defeats, was therefore make-or-break for my style of captaincy.

Bernie Fraser of New Zealand shows his pace. His try against the South of Scotland in October 1983 impressed Peter Brown enormously.

With only a short time to go England were comfortably ahead at 15-8. We scored an unconverted try — and then came my favourite try. Ian McLauchlan set up a good ruck, scrum-half Duncan Paterson broke and headed open into the England 22. I accepted his short pass and after four quick steps threw a one-handed pass across the face of the England posts to Chris Rea who took it with a small readjustment and crossed well out. My conversion was the last kick of the game.

Eleven days later, still very full of ouselves, we whipped England 26-6 in the RFU centenary match and I continued successfully as captain for another full year.

MOST MEMORABLE TRY WITNESSED
South of Scotland (9) v New Zealand (30), Galashiels, 29.10.1983

Bernie Fraser's try after 20 minutes helped the All Blacks into their stride and they went on to win easily. I nominate it because in my coaching role at Gala I spend all my time tutoring basic handling and kicking skills, but young and mature players alike, though talented, do not seem to put in the necessary hours of repetitive practice essential to produce under pressure the deliberate and controlled kick or pass which leaves the opposition wide open — as on this occasion.

The All Blacks were scrummaging in attack on the South's 22-line close to the right touch-line, their backs wide across the whole field with the full-back deep and Fraser very far out on the left. Scrummage ball was slowly delivered, the half-back passed long and well on the open side to his first five-eighth who transferred immediately, without a step, to the second five-eighth. He ran a few paces across field, feinting to link with the full-back coming up flat inside the wing but instead kicking left-footed over the now lured-up three-quarter line of the South, whose full-back was also sprinting forward and across to mark his opposite number. Bernie Fraser was already in full stride having anticipated the kick and was able to fall unchallenged on the ball as it rolled nicely over the South's goal line. The set-piece ball had been of only average quality, but two excellent passes and the delayed, controlled kick set up the try. All so simple . . .

Norman Bruce
(Blackheath, the Army, London Scottish & Scotland)
31 caps for Scotland (1958-64) as a hooker. Now lives near Oswestry, Shropshire.

MOST MEMORABLE TRY SCORED
Scotland (6) v Wales (5), Murrayfield, 7.2.1959

The situation was tense with Scotland defending close to our line when our pack came away in a controlled dribble, Ken Smith in the van. The Welsh backs seemed to have gone into slow motion and failed to respond quickly to the developing threat. Gordon Waddell eventually picked up, with myself tracking him down the touch-line. The final pass was given some 20 yards our — and at the corner flag I went down under Terry Davies's tackle as if pole-axed but the try which won Scotland the match was there for history to see and marvel over!

MOST MEMORABLE TRY WITNESSED
Transvaal (17) v Barbarians (17), Johannesburg, 10.5.1958

With only minutes to go the Baa-Baas were behind, needing three points for a draw, five for victory — and Tony O'Reilly was nearing the end of a long, dramatic run out of defence, preparing to run around from Transvaal's corner flag to the posts for an easy conversion. Here he tripped over some cameramen who had taken up position on the in-goal area and as a result touched the ball down, the try being awarded near touch. The conversion was missed and we had to settle for a draw.

That is the sort of incident which certainly doesn't happen often in top Rugby. However, it cost us the match and has stuck in my mind.

Gert Brynard

(Western Province & South Africa)
7 Tests for South Africa (1965-68) as a wing.
Now lives in Mtunzini, South Africa.

MOST MEMORABLE TRY SCORED
New Zealand (16) v South Africa (19),
Christchurch, 4.9.1965

When we ran onto a wet and slippery Lancaster Park, the Springboks had lost seven Tests in a row, including the first two in the series by 6-3 and 13-0, and our morale was very low. John Gainsford scored a try in the first half and, despite the All Blacks' 16-3 interval lead, we still felt we were in with a chance — with some justification as it turned out, for I scored immediately on the resumption, Gainsford got another which Naude converted and suddenly we were only 16-11 behind. It was at this point that my favourite try came.

I received the ball from Mannetjies Roux on the New Zealand 25 some 20 yards from touch. Realizing that we needed five points to tie the scores, and that my chances of outsprinting the speedy Bill Birtwhistle to the corner were just as slim as going inside, I just took off straight for the posts — but found my path blocked by what looked to me like a wall of players (though in fact there were only three, Moreton, Laidlaw and Williment).

That was when I stopped thinking and just tried to dive over their heads. It felt like they were holding me in the air for minutes, but I managed to slot the ball just beside an upright and Tiny Naude put over the easy conversion for 16-16.

Just on full time Naude put over a great penalty from touch to win the match.

MOST MEMORABLE PARTICIPATION IN TRIES
Northern Transvaal v Western Province, Pretoria,
Currie Cup 1964

Of the many great and wonderful tries I have seen two will remain for ever in my memory, both scored on this day by the same player and virtually identical.

The occasion was a Currie Cup final on Northern Transvaal's home ground where they had beaten us earlier in the season by 29-6. The odds against Western Province lengthened soon after the start when Jannie Engelbrecht was late tackled and suffered a bad break of the left collarbone. No replacements were allowed in those days, but to remove one player from a pack up against opponents like Mof Myburgh, Frik du Preez and Louis Smidt would have left our forwards with no hope; so although Jannie was in absolute agony, Doug Hopwood, our skipper, begged him to stay on. It was in the second half that he got his two memorable tries.

The first followed an entry into the line by myself from the left wing, the second an open-side break by scrum-half Dirkie de Vos. On both occasions we had to feather-pass the ball to Engelbrecht since he could use only his right arm. Each time he took the ball beautifully under the good arm and, after swerving around full-back Martin Grundlingh, raced away for 50 yards chased by his opposite number Ernest du Plessis, at that time rated the fastest Rugby player in South Africa. But Jannie was running faster than I ever saw any other human being on a Rugby field, his face contorted with pain, his left arm hanging like the broken wing of a bird. Both times he just fell in a heap over the line with du Plessis around his ankles.

Jannie carried on to become one of South Africa's greatest wings — and Western Province won the Currie Cup!

Robert (Bob) Burgess

(Manawatu & New Zealand)
7 Tests for New Zealand (1971-73) as first
five-eighth.
Now lives in Palmerston North, New Zealand.

*Bob Burgess in full cry. The All Black winger remembers with
pride his second try of the Christchurch test of 1971 against the
British Lions – an example of 'classic simplicity'.*

MOST MEMORABLE TRY SCORED
**New Zealand (22) v British Isles (12),
Christchurch, 10.7.1971**

The try was scored towards the end of the game.
New Zealand won a ruck within the Lions' 25,
just to the left of the posts. From the right-hand
side of the field I ran diagonally across the base
of the ruck in a straight line towards the Lions'
right-wing, Gerald Davies. All Black scrum half
Sid Going popped the ball into my hands just as
I brushed past him, and his timing allowed me,
running at full speed, to outflank the opposing
loose forwards. With New Zealand wing Bryan
Williams on my left I found Gerald hanging
back — and myself crossing the line.

I choose this try for its classic simplicity. My
high-school coach had taught me to run the
blind side in this way: 'Go hard, straight, close to
the base of scrum or ruck.' With the rest of the
team playing their parts — the forwards driving
ahead and committing the opposing pack, the
half-back timing his pass, and the blind-side
wing running parallel ready for a pass should
his opposite number move in to take me — I was
able to score an exact copy of the try with which
I opened the scoring in the first half.

MOST MEMORABLE TRY WITNESSED
**New Zealand Universities (6) v British Isles (27),
Wellington, 7.7.1971**

After the British Isles won a scrum on the
Universities' 25, the ball was sent to Barry John,
in front of the posts and well positioned to drop
a goal. Several of our players, myself and
open-side flanker Alex Matheson included,
charged at John to prevent three points. He
stopped, feinted with a shrug of his shoulders
and rolling of his eyes, and glided past the
erstwhile defence as it lay spreadeagled on the
ground. Sheer magic!

Mike Burton

(Gloucester, England & British Isles)
17 caps for England (1972-78) as a prop-forward.
Now lives near Gloucester.

MOST MEMORABLE TRY WITNESSED
England (12) v Ireland (16), Twickenham, 12.2.1972

The try I choose was scored by Ireland against England during my second international match — and I single it out because it was the biggest con I ever saw on a Rugby field.

My first cap had been against Wales two weeks earlier. We had lost 12-6, which made our Irish encounter even more important. In the week leading up to the game we heard stories about the Irish training on Guinness, then running twice around Barry ('I don't have to train, do I?') McGann, the most genial of stand-off halves; and during our pre-match pep-talk we had been warned that the Irish always played well towards the Wimpey advert at the end of the RFU ground (it wasn't until half-time that I realized there were Wimpey signs at both ends!).

Despite all this, until close to the end we led an Irish XV containing all-time greats like Willie John McBridge, Ray McLoughlin and Mike Gibson — England had one or two handy lads too, Bob Hiller and David Duckham among them. I couldn't for the life of me have told you the score as we got down inside our own 22 for what had to be the last scrum of the game, but I knew that Ireland were behind. Their hooker Ken Kennedy struck sweetly on his own put-in and with my head buried in the scrum I saw their scrum half collect the ball and heard the dull thud that told me he'd dive-passed. By the time I had straightened up McGann was about to deliver the ball to one Kevin Flynn, a diminutive centre: he had been around for some time, I seemed to remember, which isn't to say he was old and past his best, but I would not have put much money on him in a race against his opposite number, England's brilliant David Duckham. As McGann shaped to give the pass Flynn screamed 'inside!' as if to take a crash ball. In that split second McGann threw a floater of a pass right across the front of Duckham who,

had he been upright, would have gathered and gone the length of the field, but he was by now committed and already moving to take Flynn on the inside.

I remember thinking, 'Christ, McGann's messed this up' because he leaned away like a public-school centre to make his pass and, with Flynn apparently coming inside, I had visions of disaster for Ireland with the ball going loose behind their three-quarter line. But I needn't have worried, for Flynn, without doing anything fancy at all, took the pass and was away past the luckless Duckham who by this time was on his hands and knees facing the opposite way. With the English cover closing fast Flynn passed to the unmarked Gibson who appeared outside him and cantered in to score the winning try.

Why should I rate this the most memorable of all? Because it came when it mattered most to the team that scored it. And the devious Irishman who perpetrated the thing had obviously planned it down to the last detail.

A few weeks later on a Barbarians' tour in South Wales I had the pleasure of sharing a room with the redoubtable Flynn. He told me that as McGann cocked most things up there was no point in confusing him too much, so they had used one plan only: that was for Flynn to shout 'inside' when he wanted a long, floating pass and 'outside' when he required a short, sharp pass to latch onto and crash through.

'So,' I said, 'you knew full well when you shouted "inside" that you would get a long, floating pass, so you drifted wide on the tackler's outside, did you?'

'Well, that was the plan,' Flynn admitted almost seriously. But then, with his face cracking into a wide smile, 'to tell ye the truth, I didn't know what the hell was going to happen!'

Kevin Flynn, his face a mixture of determination and delight, leaves the English defence in tatters. Mike Gibson is not far behind, ready to take the pass and score 'the biggest con' Mike Burton ever saw.

E. T. (Eddie) Butler

(Pontypool, Wales & British Isles)
15 caps for Wales (1980-84) as a number eight forward.
Now lives in Bassaleg, Gwent.

MOST MEMORABLE TRY SCORED
Wales (18) v Scotland (34), Cardiff, 20.3.1982

A first try for one's country is always memorable, even though mine was scored in a losing side. Scotland got the bit between their teeth on this day and scorched away to a first victory in ten visits to Cardiff Arms Park.

I scored following a typical peel into the midfield from a line-out by my Pontypool clubmate Graham Price. Some swift interpassing followed and a path to the line opened up. Besides jubilation at getting the try my other reaction was to look up at the scoreboard and think, 'We could still win this!' But with Wales 27-18 down even after the conversion by Gwyn Evans I was, sadly, being over-optimistic and it was Scotland who came back to score seven more points.

MOST MEMORABLE PARTICIPATION IN TRY
Scotland (15) v Wales (19), Murrayfield, 19.2.1983

The following year found Wales, naturally, bent on revenge in Murrayfield with Scotland competing for dear life on their home ground. Midway through the second half we held a four-point lead which tremendous Scottish pressure was threatening to wipe out any moment. Then came a masterly try in the best Welsh tradition.

Rather than kick for touch on our 22 Malcolm Dacey gave Clive Rees a pass with a yard or two to move in. Our wing left several Scots for dead as he brought the ball up on our left to half-way where he found that Dacey had stayed in close support. Forwards, including myself, were there too, and immediately on our right the three-quarters in perfect formation. David Richards, Rob Ackerman and Mark Wyatt combined to send Elgan Rees over for a score that brought the house down. It encouraged us to hold on for victory in the face of Scotland's final counter-offensive.

Jeff Butterfield

(Northampton, England & British Isles)
28 caps for England (1953-59), 4 Tests for British Isles (1955) as a centre.
Now lives in London.

MOST MEMORABLE TRY SCORED
South Africa (22) v British Isles (23), Johannesburg, 6.8.1955

After 20 minutes of this game we — that is, Cliff Morgan and myself — decided to run the ball. Our endeavour was always to pass to the wings, so we put a few passes the way of Cecil Pedlow and Tony O'Reilly which had the defence under stress. When the moment was ripe I sold dummies to the South African centres and with a sharp change of direction scored between the posts.

MOST MEMORABLE PARTICIPATION IN TRY
England (9) v Australia (6), Twickenham, 1.2.1958

We were into extra time by many minutes, thanks to numerous casualties on our side, with the score 6-6. Phil Horrocks-Taylor had gone off injured before half-time, so I had moved to stand-off half and Peter Robbins had left the pack to play at centre. Our only way to score was to pass the ball to the wings, which we did repeatedly. Ultimately, in the last move of the match, Peter Jackson evaded a very tired cover defence to score at the corner for a remarkable win.

Ollie Campbell

(Old Belvedere, Ireland & British Isles)
24 caps for Ireland (1976-84), 7 Tests for the British Isles (1980-83) as a stand-off half and occasional centre.
Now lives in Malahide, Co. Dublin.

MOST MEMORABLE PARTICIPATION IN TRIES
Ireland (20) v Wales (12), Dublin, 23.1.1982

After a scrummage I attacked down the narrow side and threw a few dummies which got me past the Welsh back row. Confronted by the full-back I sent a pass to our left-wing Moss Finn who went over in the corner.

This set Ireland up for a victory which took us over the first hurdle in what turned out to be a Triple Crown year. It also showed that I could do something other than just kick!

South African Invitation XV (19) v British Isles (22), Potchefstroom, 21.5.1980

Rugby is, among other things, about containing and support play and the try which saved this game for the Lions was about both. It began with David Richards's running out of defence and ended 33 passes later with Mike Slemen's touch-down.

I choose this try because Rugby is a team game and if ever a try was scored by a team, this was it.

Mike Slemen – he touched down for the Lions against a South African Invitation XV in May 1980 after a move of 33 passes. 'If ever a try was scored by a team – this was it.'

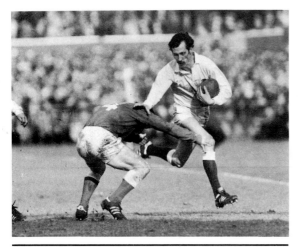

Johan Claassen

(Western Transvaal & South Africa)
28 caps for South Africa (1955-62) as a lock-forward.
Now lives at Potchefstroom, South Africa.

MOST MEMORABLE TRY SCORED
South Africa (34) v British Isles (14), Bloemfontein, 12.9.1962

As a lock-forward I didn't score a bunch of tries. But there is one I favour more than the others — for sentimental reasons: because it was the very last I scored and it happened in my last Test match.

The Springboks got possession at a line-out near half-way and started a move into midfield. Clever short passing and ultra-close support between the forwards gained us a lot of ground. The British Isles, however, managed to halt us about 15 yards short of the goal-line, where a maul developed. The ball came into my possession and I drove my way across.

I choose this try not just for the reasons stated above, but also because it showed that forwards can start a move and round it off. That is something a back-line cannot do.

MOST MEMORABLE TRY WITNESSED
New South Wales (3) v South Africa (25), Sydney, 10.7.1971

Ian McCallum started the try from within his own 25, reaching out to retrieve an impossible ball as it floated towards the Members' stand and just managing to keep his balance. Deciding to open up he moved infield to his left where wing Hannes Viljoen took over and further unsettled an already shaken defence before feeding the Springbok skipper Hannes Marais.

He gained a lot more ground and the forwards, now in command, swept infield where Marais shovelled a pass to Piet Greyling. In support of him was newcomer Morne de Plessis who took the ball with outstretched arms ten yards out and shot over at the corner. A magnificent try!

M. J. Campbell-Lamerton

*(Halifax, the Army, London Scottish, Scotland &
British Isles)*
23 caps for Scotland (1961-66), 8 Tests for British
Isles (1962-66) as a lock-forward and number eight.
Now lives in Camberley, Surrey.

MOST MEMORABLE TRY SCORED
South Africa (34) v British Isles (14), Bloemfontein, 26.8.1962

The last five minutes of the final Test had
arrived, with South Africa in a rampant mood.
Bryn Meredith collected the ball quickly to
throw in at a line-out on the Springboks' 25 and,
while Willie John McBride acted as though the
ball was destined for the front, sent an excellent
long ball to me at the tail. I jumped in front of
South Africa's number eight, Doug Hopwood,
caught the ball and dummied to Lions' scrum
half Dickie Jeeps.

Then I found a gap in the line between
Hopwood and Frik du Preez and heard Bill
Mulcahy yell, 'Go on your own!' So I went —
bowling over the opposition's scrum-half Piet
Vys and a flanker, Johannes Botha, to score.

I choose this try because it was scored in a
Test match. It may not have been a spectacular
one but it was an act of defiance and gave our
captain Arthur Smith, who was injured on the
bench, something to cheer about especially
when the home crowd went silent. It showed
that we were prepared to fight to the end, and it
proved to me how our senior players like
Meredith, Jeeps and Mulcahy were always alive
to an opportunity.

MOST MEMORABLE PARTICIPATION IN TRY
Western Province (13) v British Isles (21), Cape Town, 14.7.1962

The score was 13-13 in a thrilling match when
Western Province were caught offside at a
scrum on their 25. Our skipper, Arthur Smith,
bravely decided not to call for a kick at goal,
Dickie Jeeps instead taking a tapped penalty. He
passed to Keith Rowlands, who charged forward and sent a flipped pass to Haydn Morgan.
Alun Pask finally came storming up on the
outside to take his pass and squeeze in brilliantly
at the corner flag.

I choose this try because it capped one of
those magic moments when good passing, sensi-
ble support play and speed of thought paid off.
The spectators gave a standing ovation to a
score which was a turning-point; after it we went
from strength to strength.

Scotland may have brought Gerald Davies to his knees but ...

Terry Cobner

(Pontypool, Wales & British Isles)
19 caps for Wales (1974-78), 3 Tests for the British
Isles (1977) as a flanker.
Now lives in Pontypool, Gwent.

MOST MEMORABLE TRY SCORED
Wales (6) v Scotland (0), Cardiff, 19.1.1974

To score for Wales on one's debut is reason
enough for choosing a particular try. It came
after close support of a Gerald Davies break.
Cutting in from the right he wrong-footed
several Scots defenders before being tackled by
the full-back. I took the ball as he bobbed it up
and scored the only try of the game.

In all honesty I thought a Welsh place had
passed me by and the first cap came late in my
playing career. That was a great thrill, but to
score as well was marvellous.

MOST MEMORABLE PARTICIPATION IN TRY
Scotland (9) v Wales (18), Murrayfield, 19.3.1977

The try run in by Phil Bennett was remarkable
by any standards. But it also said a lot about the
Welsh team of that era and its ability to respond
positively whatever the circumstances.

We had soaked up a great deal of Scottish
pressure, weathering the storm. It showed
courage and character to come out of defence
and score a decisive try.

*... Terry Cobner is on hand to collect the ball and storm over for
a try in his international debut.*

Peter Cranmer

(Moseley & England)
16 caps for England (1934-38) as a centre.
Now lives at Walsall, Staffordshire.

MOST MEMORABLE PARTICIPATION IN TRIES
England (13) v New Zealand (0), Twickenham, 4.1.1936

Just before the interval I made a break and
looked to the right for England's Russian
prince, Alex Obolensky, who had already scored
one try. I couldn't see him — there were two All
Blacks in between us — so I passed to Candler.
Obo came inside from our right, took the ball
from Candler and continued running to outpace the defence and score on our left.

It was the height of daring and deserved to be
crowned with a try. Hal Sever, our other wing,
said he thought Obo didn't quite know where to
go and just kept on until he crossed the line!

England (9) v Ireland (8), Twickenham, 13.2.1937

I bracket the try scored by Hal Sever with that of
Andy Hancock against Scotland in 1965 when
the Northampton wing received the ball on the
England left just short of the 25 and kept
running down the touch-line, beating off all
defenders as they came across to him. I was
summing up on radio and saw it all with a bird's
eye view.

In 1937 I passed to Sever in almost the same
position, and his running was identical. However, he reached the line with Ireland's full-back
and a wing on his back. Tremendous strength!

Danie Craven

(Western Province & South Africa
16 Tests for South Africa (1931-38) as a
scrum-half.
Now lives in Stellenbosch, South Africa.

MOST MEMORABLE TRIES WITNESSED
South Africa (22) v British Isles (23), Johannesburg, 6.8.1955

The tourists had done extremely well in the
run-up to this first Test and were hot favourites.
But the Springboks began so well that it looked
as if against the odds they might swamp the
Lions. A few minutes before half-time they led
11-3.

Then came the turning point which every
match has. Against the run of play Cliff Morgan
broke, only to be halted by a cover defence
which contained such outstanding players as
Basie van Wyk, Stephen Fry and Dan Retief.
Morgan gave to Jeff Butterfield who had Tony
O'Reilly outside him on the wing. In a flash the
centre summed up the position and realized
that the overlap which was there would not help
O'Reilly notwithstanding his terrific speed. Instead of passing he cut in behind the opposition
backs.

The ball, however, had reached him slightly
to his rear, and he had caught it behind his hip.
Despite this Butterfield did not slow down,
running flat out with the ball behind his back,
working it over during his run from one side to
the other. He rounded off his break by scoring
between the posts.

His handling had been superb, as was his
summing-up of the situation and the course of
action he chose. This try was the death knell for
South Africa and put paid to my hopes of
winning the Test in my capacity as Springbok
coach.

France (3) v South Africa (25), Paris, 16.2.1952

I was Assistant Manager of the 1951-52 Springboks in Britain and France and also coached
them. This second memorable try was the last of
a tour in which 30 matches were won including
all five Tests and only one lost, to London
Counties.

From a scrum on their 25 South Africa

launched an attack through the three-quarters,
the ball eventually reaching 'Chum' Ochse who
got around his opposite number. When cut off
he sent the ball inside for the forwards to handle
and then head back for the same sector of the
field. Ochse was still out of action but Paul
Johnstone had cut across to link with the
forwards again. They made ground and, for a
third time, moved the ball to the left wing
where, this time, Ochse took the pass. His
cross-kick landed in front of the whole Springbok pack, and Basie van Wyk scored the try.

John Currie

(Bristol & England)
25 caps for England (1956-62) as a lock-forward.
Now lives at High Wycombe, Buckinghamshire.

MOST MEMORABLE PARTICIPATION IN TRY
England (9) v Australia (6), Twickenham, 1.2.1958

Some eight or nine minutes into injury time the scores were level at 6-6. It had been a dirty game, with three of our players laid out and Phil Horrocks-Taylor obliged to leave the field early on — but in days before replacements were allowed we battled on with 14 men.

I obtained clean possession at a line-out, and the ball went quickly along the three-quarters (who included an emergency centre in our flanker Peter Robbins) to Peter Jackson on the right wing. Receiving the ball on the half-way line he went outside his man, inside a covering centre and finally outside the Wallaby full-back, Lenehan, to score at the corner.

This was a really great try, as Australia were defending as if their lives depended on it to get the draw.

MOST MEMORABLE TRY WITNESSED
England (3) v Scotland (3), Twickenham, 20.3.1965

I was in the enclosure at Twickenham and with five minutes of the game left England were 3-0 down. I was about to pay my debts to three nearby Scotsmen when one said, 'I will believe a win when I see it — something unusual always happens in the Calcutta Cup match.' Two minutes later in the England 25 Mike Weston gave the ball to Andy Hancock who set off to run the whole length of the field to score an equalizing try.

As with the Jackson try it takes that extra something to break down a defence and come from behind late in a game, since the determination of the side in the lead at that time is heightened.

Claude Davey

(Swansea & Wales)
23 caps for Wales (1930-38) as a centre.
Now lives in Brecon, Powys.

MOST MEMORABLE TRY SCORED
Swansea (11) v New Zealand (3), Swansea, 28.9.1935

Some 30 minutes into the match the ball reached Haydn Tanner from a line-out near half-way. He passed beautifully to Willie Davies, who made a half break. As I received his pass I was up to full speed and could thus race away to the line unopposed.

I choose this try because it combined perfect understanding between two players with perfect timing. Also it brought about the first-ever defeat of an All Black XV by a club side (and only the second reverse for New Zealand in Britain since 1905). It is a reminder of the great display by the two schoolboys at half-back, Haydn Tanner and Willie Davies. And, moreover, some critics were kind enough to describe it as the try of a lifetime!

MOST MEMORABLE TRY WITNESSED
Wales (35) v Scotland (12), Cardiff, 5.2.1972

This has to be Gareth Edwards's brilliant second try, which I choose because it included the very best aspects of Rugby, and it showed imagination combined with great speed and intense concentration.

Gareth Davies in typical action. He remembers vividly the try he scored in injury time to win the game for Wales/England against Scotland/Ireland in November 1980.

Gareth Davies
(Cardiff, Wales & British Isles)
18 caps for Wales (1978-82), 1 Test for British Isles (1980) as a stand-off half.
Now lives in Cardiff, South Glamorgan.

MOST MEMORABLE TRY SCORED
Wales/England (37) v Scotland/Ireland (33), Cardiff, 29.11.1980

The game had moved into injury time and Wales/England were not only trailing by two points but also defending desperately on our own line. Then, from a scrummage, Terry Holmes made a marvellous break, sold a dummy, and kicked ahead into the Scotland/Ireland half. Fast following-up secured the second phase for us and I eventually received a scoring pass to get in at the posts. I converted the try to seal our triumph.

Any winning try is memorable, especially if it is scored on National Ground, Cardiff Arms Park, in a big match!

MOST MEMORABLE TRY WITNESSED
South African Invitation XV (19) v British Isles (22), Potchefstroom, 21.5.1980

Mike Slemen was the eventual scorer after a stunning period of interpassing between backs and forwards.

I was present to see the Barbarians' opening try against New Zealand at Cardiff in 1973, but Slemen's try surpassed that. It was scored against top-class opposition and rounded off almost two minutes of continuous play, an achievement in itself.

Mervyn Davies

(London Welsh, Swansea, Wales & British Isles)
38 caps for Wales (1969-76), 8 Tests for British Isles (1971-74) as a number eight.
Now lives in Swansea, West Glamorgan.

MOST MEMORABLE TRY SCORED
Barbarians (13) v New Zealand (13), Twickenham, 30.11.1974

I am a great admirer of New Zealand Rugby, especially its forward play, and was never on a winning side against the All Blacks in Britain. This day, I nearly achieved that aim with a try which may have looked like a short-range job but which actually climaxed a run of some 60 metres in support of our speedy backs.

The try remained unconverted. None the less, on what was to be the last occasion for me to play against New Zealand, it gave me great satisfaction to deny the All Blacks victory!

MOST MEMORABLE TRY WITNESSED
New Zealand (22) v British Isles (12), Christchurch, 10.7.1984

As a back-row forward Ian Kirkpatrick was without equal. For a big man he was very agile and extremely quick, virtues which he demonstrated with his try in this match.

First he broke away from a maul on the half-way line. Then he burst through several tackles before racing some 40 yards to touch down under the posts, outstripping the Lions' three-quarter line on his way.

I always dreamed of scoring a try like that!

(below and following two pages)
Anatomy of a try – Mervyn Davies shows exceptional power and determination to force his way through All Black Andy Leslie for a try which helped ensure a draw for the Barbarians.

W. P. C. (Phil) Davies

(Harlequins, England & British Isles)
11 caps for England (1953-58), 3 Tests for British Isles (1955) as a centre.
Now lives in Cheltenham, Gloucestershire.

MOST MEMORABLE PARTICIPATION IN TRY
South Africa (22) v British Isles (23), Johannesburg, 6.8.1955

The first try of a four-Test series is always memorable. After ten minutes Tony O'Reilly threw in to a line-out on the Lions' right (and then continued addressing the crowd on the rights of persecuted minorities). There was a two-handed catch, and the ball reached me via Dickie Jeeps and Cliff Morgan. My outside swerve past van Vollenhoven broke the defence and, though my pass to Jeff Butterfield was not a good one he just held it, drew the Springbok full-back and put Cecil Pedlow in at the corner.

I choose this try because we won the Test and a relatively unknown group who set out with little Press coverage thus came of age; because it was seen by a world record crowd estimated at 100,000; and because I was 27 that day!

MOST MEMORABLE TRY WITNESSED
England (9) v Australia (6), Twickenham, 1.2.1958

Malcolm Phillips, who had taken over from me in the England midfield, gave right-wing Peter Jackson the ball with room to move about 30 yards out. The wing beat three men with will o' the wisp running to score at the corner in injury time and win the match.

Peter Jackson, so often unstoppable inside the 25, is probably the only man who could have scored that try. It also sticks in my memory because it dealt the Australians justice on the day — their tactics were so crude that they did not deserve victory.

John Dawes

(London Welsh, Wales & British Lions)
22 caps for Wales (1964-71), 4 Tests for the British Isles (1971) as a centre.
Now lives in Cardiff.

MOST MEMORABLE TRY SCORED:
Ireland (6) v Wales (15), Dublin, 7.3.1964

A first game for one's country is always memorable, and mine was made more so by scoring one of the three Welsh tries. It came, I recall, from a fairly orthodox three-quarter movement in which the ball was moved left to the tearaway Peter Rees. He beat his man on the outside but was channelled towards touch by Ireland's full back Keogh. I had kept running inside him, however, and was well placed at the vital moment to accept a return pass and cross the line from short range.

In retrospect, this was a rare victory to have gained. Wales had to wait until 1976 to win again at Lansdowne Road.

MOST MEMORABLE PARTICIPATION IN TRY:
Hawke's Bay (6) v British Isles (25), Napier, 14.7.1971

Hawke's Bay came at the Lions very hard, hoping to repeat New Zealand's Test victory over us a week earlier, and had taken the lead. Then, after their full-back, Bishop, had hit a post with a long drop at goal, the ball fell to J.P.R. Williams, who might have been expected to kick for touch. Instead he moved rapidly upfield and linked with a couple of us in the three-quarter line, after which the ball found its way to Mervyn Davies coming up fast along the touch-line. Finding himself cut off our number eight directed the ball infield with a pass that was not at all bad (for a forward) but unfortunately just failed to reach Gerald Davies on the full.

Controlling the ball expertly, however, 'Reames' drove it on beyond the last defenders before judging exactly the right bounce for grasping it and racing over the line for the first of the four tries he scored that day.

I pick out this try because it exemplified the style of the 1971 Lions, who would always be looking for a chance to attack even when under extreme pressure. The quality of the skills and support play was also high.

Colin Deans
(Hawick, Scotland & British Isles)
34 Tests for Scotland (1978-84) as a hooker.
Now lives at Hawick, Borders

Colin Deans scored his first and only (so far!) international try for Scotland against New Zealand in 1981.

MOST MEMORABLE TRY SCORED
New Zealand (11) v Scotland (4), Dunedin, 13.6.1981

On a very wet day the first of Scotland's two Tests against New Zealand was 60 minutes old. At a line-out on the half-way line the All Blacks' skipper Andy Dalton threw to Graeme Higginson who attempted a deflection to scrum-half Dave Loveridge but sent the ball over his head to be latched onto by Iain Paxton, playing in his first Test. He kicked the ball into my path near the touch-line. I was coming up to Stu Wilson and on the New Zealand 22 managed to dribble past him. He now had to turn, while I was in full flight and able to win the race for the touch-down.

I choose this try because it was my first (and, to date, only) international try — and because it was scored against the All Blacks.

MOST MEMORABLE PARTICIPATION IN TRY
Wales (18) v Scotland (34), Cardiff, 20.3.1982

About 15 minutes into this game Scotland were trailing 3-0 and had spent most of the time defending. Wales whipped the ball to Gareth Davies who, from just outside our 22, kicked for the corner. Here the bounce was bad for Wales, kind to Scotland. Roger Baird, possibly the fastest man in Scottish Rugby in the early eighties, took the ball at speed, beat the Welsh backs who were in attacking formation, raced to the half-way line and, drawing the full-back, passed inside to Iain Paxton. He was nailed from behind by Clive Rees but managed to pass inside to Alan Tomes who was being overhauled near the Welsh line by Gareth Davies but had Jim Calder outside him and myself on the inside. Alan passed the wrong way — to Jim! — but we got the try.

We went on to score five that day. I choose this first one because it came from a defensive position on our line. It showed that Scotland were capable of attacking and scoring from anywhere.

Lewis G. Dick

(Loughborough Colleges, Jordanhill, Swansea & Scotland)
14 caps for Scotland (1972-77) as a wing.
Now lives in Cheltenham, Gloucestershire.

MOST MEMORABLE TRY SCORED
Scotland (10) v Australia (3), Murrayfield, 6.12.1975

International matches are played at such a frantic pace and with such intense concentration that few recollections of particular incidents are clear. Thus it is safer to rely on the accounts of Pressmen who covered the game for details of the blind-side move whereby Douglas Morgan, Ian McGeechan and Bruce Hay combined to send me in for a try.

What I remember most vividly, however, is the Australian cover almost nailing me at the corner as the ball was grounded. The corner flag crashed over, referee Johnny Johnson raised his arm heavenward signalling a try, and the Wallabies vehemently denied its legality.

Scotland's forward power at the time meant that strategy revolved around the pack, the three-quarters playing a secondary role. The try I have chosen was thus gratifying as an illustration that Scottish backs — men like Irvine, McGeechan, Renwick and Hay — could make an important contribution. It was rewarding for me, as wing, to score this kind of try. And, finally, it has to be admitted that it was the first registered by Scotland in over six hours of international Rugby!

MOST MEMORABLE TRY WITNESSED
Wales (35) v Scotland (12), Cardiff, 5.2.1972

On this day Gareth Edwards broke from inside the Welsh half, chipped the ball over the head of our full-back, and raced on to beat the cover and score at the corner.

In a sense I participated in the try since I threw the ball in at the initial line-out from which the Welsh won possession. It was my first touch of the ball in an international, having been called on as a replacement for Alistair Biggar midway through the second half. Any player who has come on in this way especially in an international match, will know how difficult it is to enter the fray 'cold'.

The winning of my first cap, dreamed about since schooldays, had become a reality. Further, within minutes of my first venture into the arena I had been involved in and witnessed one of the most legendary tries of all time.

David Duckham

(Coventry, England & British Isles).
36 caps for England (1969-76), 3 Tests for British
Isles (1971) as centre and wing.
Now lives at Stratford-upon-Avon, Warwickshire.

MOST MEMORABLE TRY SCORED
Cardiff (11) v Barbarians (9), Cardiff, 13.4.1974

In an innocent-looking three-quarter movement, going left, one centre was missed with the
consequence that I received the ball early, was
able to run at my opposite number on the
Cardiff right wing and simply beat him on the
outside for pace. The only other defender, the
full-back, was also beaten on the outside because
he, naturally, thought that I would attempt to
swerve or side-step inside him. I scored near the
posts.

I choose this try because it was simple,
emanating from an ordinary piece of play. The
ball was moved quickly enabling me to have
space in which to manoeuvre. I had to do the
unexpected — and simply beat the defenders on
the outside, the traditional route all too seldom
taken these days.

MOST MEMORABLE TRY WITNESSED
England (23) v Scotland (17), Twickenham, 7.2.1981

Clive Woodward switched with Paul Dodge in
midfield on the Scottish ten-metre line and by
dummying to his forwards went past at least
three covering Scotsmen. Then he swerved and
weaved his way through the remainder of the
defence, feinted to pass to his blindside wing,
and reached the line.

This try was exceptional because of Woodward's sheer instinct and balanced running. He
could not have expected to reach the line for he
was constantly looking for a support player to
whom to pass. However, in the end a half-gap
was all he needed to exploit the situation on his
own. A superb example of individualism.

Clive Woodward of England sells a dummy ...

30

... and Scotland's Rowan and Aitken buy it comprehensively as the centre slices his way through the Scottish defence for a try which Duckham calls 'a superb example of individualism'.

Gareth Edwards

(Cardiff Training College, Cardiff, Wales & British Isles)
53 caps for Wales (1967-78), 10 Tests for the British Isles (1968-1974) as a scrum-half.
Now lives in Porthcawl, Mid Glamorgan.

MOST MEMORABLE TRY SCORED
Wales (35) v Scotland (12), Cardiff, 5.2.1972

My first try, scored from short range and converted by Barry John, seemed to lift the Welsh pack and gave us a 16-12 lead. Then came the second, which I count a particular favourite.

It began at a line-out on our 25-yard line. Mervyn Davies, at number eight, gained possession, drove forward to tie in the Scottish loose forwards and sent the ball back to me. What happened next can be divided into several stages:

(a) I decided to run with the ball up the right touch-line and see what was on. Opposing flanker Rodger Arneil was caught out of position.

(b) The adrenalin began flowing and I thought, 'I'll have a bit of a cut.' Then I looked for support but because the move took even my colleagues by surprise there was none: no sign of 'Bas' and 'Shadow' — flankers John Taylor and Dai Morris. I made up my mind to go as far as possible, maybe up to the half-way line.

(c) At that point I saw that Scotland's full-back Arthur Brown was flat-footed. But since I was beginning to tire I kicked ahead, even at this stage simply concerned to keep going forward. Brown could have stopped me with a professional foul — but to his great credit did not.

(d) It was after the kick over Brown's head that I thought for the first time of a possible try: 'I've got this far, I'm going all the way now.'

(e) As always, an element of luck played its part, the ball bobbing and curving into my path as I reached the Scottish 25 and gave it another thump. It then rolled obligingly just across the goal-line — and into my head came the incessant advice of my schoolboy mentor Bill Samuel: 'Near the line — go for it!' Some players hesitate and don't go. I did — and got the touch-down!

Bill had also said I had an 80-yard try in me. He was right — but it seemed to take an eternity. However, it was satisfying to have gone that far in front of my own crowd. I will always remember the walk back in front of them. The applause went on and on, and was as amazing as it was moving.

MOST MEMORABLE PARTICIPATION IN TRY
Scotland (9) v Wales (18), Murrayfield, 19.3.1977

Just as I can only say that my 1972 try described above was *one* of the best, so I pick out this 1977 try begun inside the Welsh 22 by J. P. R. Williams, carried on by Steve Fenwick, Gerald Davies and David Burcher, and finished off by Phil Bennett as another in the same extra-special category.

The game was typical of Wales-Scotland clashes (of which we had lost the previous two at Murrayfield, mainly through lack of discipline and the conceding of penalties). Now, with Andy Irvine at his very best, the home team was applying enormous pressure and dragging us from side to side of the field as they strove to take the lead. It was typical of the Welsh team of the day that it weathered the storm before hitting back through the one faint opportunity that presented itself. That is something all good teams must recognize and take, often turning defence into attack.

I watched and clapped from a distance and felt that if anything deserved a Triple Crown, Phil's try did. We won in style.

(opposite)
Gareth Edwards: lethal at short range, he recalls with greatest satisfaction a try which he scored against Scotland in 1972 after receiving the ball near his own 25 line. He just kept going.

R. T. (Bob) Evans

(Newport, Wales & British Isles)
10 caps for Wales (1947-51), 6 Tests for British
Isles (1950) as a flanker.
Now lives in Abergavenny, Gwent.

MOST MEMORABLE PARTICIPATION IN TRIES
England (5) v Wales (11), Twickenham, 21.1.1950

England had taken an early five-point lead. Just
before half-time the unpredictable Lewis Jones,
playing at full-back in his first international
match, caught a loose ball near half-way and
began a long zig-zag run to link with his
forwards. I received the ball from Roy John
near the right touch-line before passing to a
team-mate whom I expected to be wing Ken
Jones. To my astonishment I found I was giving
the ball to prop-forward Cliff Davies who had
raced up behind me. He crossed for three vital
points. From then on it was all Wales, and a
further try by Ray Cale, with a conversion and
penalty by Lewis Jones, gave us victory.

I have always looked upon Twickenham as
my favourite ground and this win, I believe,
secured places for twelve of the Welsh team in
the first post-War British Isles tour party to
Australia and New Zealand. For Cliff Davies's
try contributed to the high standard and flowing style of Rugby played by Wales in the three
remaining — and successful — international
matches that year.

Cardiff (3) v Newport (8), Cardiff, 17.2.1951

This game was watched by 48,500, a world
record for a club match, and had the flavour of
an international. Newport, enjoying a run of 36
matches without defeat, had won the first two of
the annual four-match series with Cardiff and
were hopeful that 1950-51 would bring the
coveted quartet of victories which they had not
previously achieved.

Cardiff led 3-0 at half-time, having played
with the wind, but despite gaining this advantage after changing ends we could make no
headway. Then, ten minutes from time, Ken
Jones drove the ball through with the Newport
pack in attendance. Derek Murphy had raced
across to cover from the Cardiff right wing but
after gathering he kicked high into the open —

and right into the welcoming hands of centre
Bryn Williams. He raced away and put John
Lane over at the posts. Ben Edwards's conver-
sion gave us a lead we were not to lose.

As the conversion went over the heavens
opened and down poured the biggest hailstones
imaginable! I can still see Jack Matthews trying
in vain to shelter his thickset frame behind a
goalpost as the bombardment persisted.

We failed to record our four wins over
Cardiff, however, for the final encounter a
fortnight later was drawn.

Okey Geffin

(Transvaal & South Africa)
7 caps for South Africa (1949-52) as a prop-forward.
Now lives in Sandton, South Africa.

J. S. (Gerrie) Germishuys

(Orange Free State, Transvaal & South Africa)
20 Tests for South Africa (1974-81) as a wing.
Now lives in Johannesburg, South Africa.

MOST MEMORABLE PARTICIPATION IN TRIES
Scotland (0) v South Africa (44), Murrayfield, 10.11.1951

During the first half the Scottish forwards were dribbling the ball and had reached a point about 30 yards from our line. The crowd were urging, 'Feet, Scotland, feet!' — and as a player in those days you knew what that meant. Finding myself almost the last line of defence I fell on the ball. Quite a few kicks in the ribs later our forwards swarmed around to heel the ball, which was passed all along the line to our wing. He cross-kicked and I was up to catch the ball, run past two defenders and pass inside. Again all our backs handled and we scored a try.

My first Test for the Springboks overseas was thus memorable to me for having stopped the Scottish rush and then handled the ball in the build-up to our try. Later we scored eight more tries, of which I converted seven.

South Africa (12) v New Zealand (6), Johannesburg, 13.8.1969

Just outside our 25 Hannes Brewis, our stand-off half, had caught a miskick for touch by Bob Scott. He turned as if to attempt a dropped goal. The whole of the New Zealand team stopped. In that split second Brewis saw a gap and made for the line. Realizing the danger a number of All Blacks attempted to tackle him but in vain. He crossed the line for a try which sent the crowd mad — we only scored three in the whole four-Test series!

MOST MEMORABLE TRY SCORED
South Africa (26) v British Isles (22), Cape Town, 31.5.1980

In this first Test the British Isles' full-back Andy Irvine picked up a ball inside his own 25 and kicked it deep across-field where I made a catch and began running towards the right. Gysie Pienaar took my pass, and received support from Ray Mordt and Rob Louw before the ball came back to him on the right-hand touchline. Here, pressurized by Mike Slemen and David Richards, Pienaar lobbed the ball over their heads where, having stayed with the move, I first had to jump to take the ball in one hand before running ten metres to score.

I choose this try because a wing should not be afraid to go to the opposite touch-line in search of work. Don't wait for opportunities to come — go and look for them!

Gerrie Germishuys in action against the Lions. He scored a fine try in the 1980 test at Cape Town.

S. M. (Sid) Going

(North Auckland & New Zealand)
29 Tests for New Zealand (1967-77) as a scrum-half.
Now lives in Maromaku, New Zealand.

MOST MEMORABLE TRY SCORED
Scotland (9) v New Zealand (14), Murrayfield, 16.12.1972

This game had moved into injury time, but the All Blacks' lead was still only 10-9. Then, close to the half-way line, I anticipated a pass about to be given by Alistair McHarg and managed to bring off an interception. Scotland, committed to attack, were taken by surprise and I covered 50 metres for a very vital try.

I choose this try because it came at a time when we really needed it to clinch victory after a very tight and hard-fought contest during which the atmosphere and tension were really something to remember.

MOST MEMORABLE PARTICIPATION IN TRY
New Zealand (22) v British Isles (12), Christchurch, 10.7.1971

I choose Ian Kirkpatrick's great try because it showed his pace, strength and ability to control the ball in hand.

Scotland's Alistair McHarg passes to New Zealand's Sid Going, who then sprinted 50 metres for an opportunist try that ensured an All Black victory.

Roger Gould

(Queensland & Australia)
12 Tests for Australia (1980-83) as a full-back.
Now lives in Ashgrove, Australia.

MOST MEMORABLE TRY SCORED
New Zealand (33) v Australia (18), Auckland, 11.9.1982

This try, scored in the first minute of the game, originated at a scrummage and had been worked out a week earlier. Our backs carried it out perfectly, a double-cut and loop designed to put the full-back into space.

I ran the try in from 35 metres, but this was the climax to a genuine team effort — that is, a perfect piece of scrummaging by the forwards yielded quick, clean ball that was passed and moved well.

MOST MEMORABLE TRY WITNESSED
Australia (9) v New Zealand (12), Brisbane, 28.6.1980

The All Blacks' try, scored when they trailed 9-6 with a quarter of an hour left, began at an unpromising line-out eight metres from their goal-line. Under pressure the first five-eighth was forced to pass rather than kick for touch. The recipient made a half-break and turned the ball inside to the forwards who set up a maul and then a ruck. Again the ball was served to the backs on the same side of the field, this time with an overlap, and when our cover finally closed on them the momentum of the attack was sustained by the forwards. Blind-side wing and full-back also got into the move, which ended with hooker Hika Reid scoring at the posts.

Although good fortune rather than design played a part at the outset, once the initial break was made the support play was excellent. The ball would have passed through five pairs of hands in the first phase and ten in the second, with some players handling twice.

J. R. H. Greenwood
(Waterloo & England)
5 caps for England (1966-69) as flanker.
Now lives in Blackburn.

MOST MEMORABLE TRY WITNESSED
Ireland (17) v England (15), Dublin, 8.2.1969

From a line-out on England's right just inside the Irish half the ball went from Wintle through Finlan to Spencer and Duckham in the centre and thence to Webb on the left wing. He cut powerfully back inside, made ground and slipped the ball outside again to Duckham who had looped around him. David fairly flew in from 30 yards out — and nearly killed himself as he plonked the ball down because in freezing conditions the pre-match straw had not been laid on the in-goal turf!

I choose this try because I was captain of England for the one and only time. Kept in contention by a phenomenal exhibition of goal-kicking from Bob Hiller (four penalty goals), it seemed as if we had done just enough to win the game. But in the event Noel Murphy sneaked over on the blind side of a maul and scored the second Irish try to beat us.

David Duckham scored a wonderful try against Ireland in 1969, but it wasn't enough to give England victory in J. R. H. Greenwood's one and only match as England's captain.

Gareth Griffiths

(Cardiff, Wales & British Isles)
12 caps for Wales (1953-57), 3 Tests for British
Isles (1955) as a wing and centre.
Now lives at Amersham, Buckinghamshire.

MOST MEMORABLE TRY SCORED
Barbarians (5) v New Zealand (19), Cardiff, 20.2.1954

For ten years I had worked hard at becoming less of a sprinter and more of a footballer. But though side-stepping off my strong right foot was easy and natural, it was less so to my left foot, especially at the speed and pace required at international level on the left wing. I had been at right centre for the Wales side which had beaten the All Blacks the previous December, and had badly dislocated my shoulder. Thus this game was a very difficult personal challenge to my fitness and self-confidence.

My try has been well described by the Pressmen of the day and in bald terms consisted of speeding onto a loose ball dropped by Bob Scott, kicking ahead, picking up the bounce and dodging my way to the posts. However, what I remember best was being able to view the whole situation at a glance and provide a controlled response to it — that is, being fully aware of what I was doing at full speed and not in the semi-conscious state which one enters during a 100-metre sprint.

It was particularly pleasing to come off my left and right feet, both a couple of times, and — having previously been so anxious about my mental state — to have the confidence to side-step in the first 20 minutes of such an important game. I could have played safe and run for the corner flag, but though I might have looked a good trier, I consider that I probably would not have scored. All in all the try was personal confirmation that my quest to become a footballing centre and not just a big, fast wing three-quarter had progressed to another level.

MOST MEMORABLE PARTICIPATION IN TRY
Wales (13) v New Zealand (8), Cardiff, 19.12.1953

This was the Ken Jones try from a Clem Thomas cross-kick which brought victory for Wales over New Zealand for a third time.

For me it represented the culmination of an afternoon of drama, exhilaration — and the personal pain and shock of a dislocated shoulder as a result of which I spent 15 minutes off the field before returning to bring us back to full strength. It was a day when I may have changed from being a boy to something approaching manhood.

Jules Guerassimoff
(Queensland & Australia)
12 Tests for Australia (1963-67) as a flanker.
Now lives in St. John's Wood, Australia.

MOST MEMORABLE TRY SCORED
Combined Services (6) v Australia (15), Twickenham, 26.12.1966

This try originated at a scrum on the Australian right some twelve yards from our opponents' corner flag. The Wallaby number eight, John O'Gorman, picked up at the back of the scrum, ran on the short side and passed inside to half-back Ken Catchpole. Confronted by the opposing number eight, he in-passed again to me and I scored unopposed.

I choose this try because it was a rehearsed move which worked to perfection. Its essence was for our blind-side flanker to remain bound on the scrummage for an extra fraction of a second which kept his opposite number down and allowed our number eight to get forward before passing inside. Then I broke from the open side and ran in support, the opposing half-back and flanker being caught in no-man's-land.

Also this was my one and only try at Twickenham.

MOST MEMORABLE PARTICIPATION IN TRY
South Africa (9) v Australia (11), Johannesburg, 24.8.1963

Australia won a long line-out 35 yards out, lock Peter Crittle peeled from the front to take a tap-down before running flat and wide to commit Springboks Riley and Gainsford and feed Dick Marks. He in turn eluded Stewart's high tackle and gave to wing John Williams who scored in the corner.

I choose this try as being a match-winner — indeed the only try of the game. Again it was a thoroughly rehearsed move in which Crittle ran wide rather than forward to draw the inside backs onto him. Marks's break outside Stewart was also memorable.

R. H. (Dickie) Guest
(Waterloo & England)
13 caps for England (1939-49) as a wing.
Now lives at Pwllheli, Gwynedd.

MOST MEMORABLE TRY SCORED
England (10) v Ireland (11), Twickenham, 14.2.1948

Midway through the second half Ireland, playing towards the South Terrace, were leading 11-5 and Barney Mullan was attempting to widen the gap with a penalty goal attempt from the 25-yard line ten yards from touch on the west side of the ground. The ball hit an upright and bounced to our prop Harry Walker who kicked for touch back in the direction of Mullan. But Jackie Kyle caught the ball and threw a long, high pass towards his three-quarters, the intended recipient being close to the middle of the field.

During this exchange I should have stayed on my right wing, but for some reason was in front of our posts. Thus on realizing Kyle's intention, I was able to run forward to intercept his pass, leaping two or three feet into the air to do so. This left me with only full-back Jack Mattson to beat and I side-stepped him before sprinting some 65 yards to the posts. Despite this, England lost narrowly, a result that was just about right.

I choose this try because it is one of very few which I can now, decades later, relive exactly as it happened by closing my eyes. Had I not intercepted, incidentally, Ireland would have scored on my unguarded wing!

MOST MEMORABLE TRY WITNESSED
England (16) v Scotland (21), Twickenham, 19.3.1938

In the second half Scotland, playing towards the North Stand, won a scrummage on the right touch-line. Tommy Dorward passed to his stand-off half, R. Wilson Shaw, who set off on a long, curving run to cross midway between posts and corner flag without a hand being laid on him.

My reason for remembering this try is that for the first time, at the age of 19, I was a travelling reserve (and nearly had to play, since our right-wing that day, Jim Unwin, was declared fit only hours before the kick-off). As a member of the squad, I was taking everything in.

John Gwilliam

(Cambridge University, Newport, Edinburgh Wanderers & Wales)
23 caps for Wales (1947-54) as lock or number eight.
Now lives at Birkenhead, Merseyside.

MOST MEMORABLE PARTICIPATION IN TRIES
England (5) v Wales (11), Twickenham, 21.1.1950

The first try I choose, which guaranteed Wales only her second victory at Twickenham in 40 years, was particularly enjoyable because of the excellent view I had of the proceedings. Lewis Jones, our 18-year-old prodigy at full-back, fielded a loose ball about 30 yards behind me and set off with his long, raking stride towards the left touch-line. He eluded most of the English three-quarters in a curving run which ended with a pass to Cliff Davies, one of our prop forwards, who was 20 yards in front of me. A miner who took size 18 in collars, Cliff was deceptively fast, having been a sprinter in his youth. Now he accepted the ball gratefully and hurtled over the line for a truly remarkable try.

England (6) v Wales (8), Twickenham, 19.1.1952

My other chosen try was scored by Ken Jones after a break by Cliff Morgan. It was notable for the giant scissors move between the two, which bewildered both sides and could only have been executed by players of exceptional speed and acceleration.

Having received the ball from Rex Willis at a scrum inside the Welsh half, Cliff Morgan showed what E. W. Swanton described as 'an electric turn of speed' to break through England's three-quarter line before veering out to the right wing. Here Ken Jones, the Olympic sprinter on our right wing, cut inside and took a perfect pass. He thus wrong-footed the whole of the opposing team, and no one laid a hand on him as he sprinted 40 yards to score.

To prove that it was not just a piece of good fortune, the pair repeated the manoeuvre later in the season at Lansdown Road, Dublin, to win the 1952 Triple Crown.

Rowe Harding

(Cambridge University, Swansea, Wales & British Isles)
17 caps for Wales (1923-28), 3 Tests for British Isles (1924) as a wing.
Now lives at Gower, West Glamorgan.

MOST MEMORABLE PARTICIPATION IN TRY
Wales (8) v Scotland (11), Cardiff, 3.2.1923

This was my second game for Wales, after an international debut in the side narrowly beaten by England at Twickenham three weeks earlier.

In the first half of the Scottish match I received the ball in midfield on the half-way line, cut through to the opposing full-back and passed to our stand-off half Clem Lewis, who scored at the posts. The try was converted and we led by eight points to six until the last five minutes when Scotland got a winning try.

I choose the try because of the personal satisfaction it afforded me and also because the game itself is historic — thanks to the try I describe next!

MOST MEMORABLE TRY WITNESSED
Wales (8) v Scotland (11), Cardiff, 3.2.1923

With five minutes to go the Welsh lead was 8-6. Then the Scottish centre A. L. Gracie, who had played brilliantly throughout, ran straight into the great Llanelli three-quarter Albert Jenkins, a powerful man and a strong tackler. Gracie knocked him over and ran in under the posts to round off a run that had come from just inside the Welsh half. His try was converted and Scotland won 11-8. A swarm of Welsh supporters ran onto the pitch and carried the Scot shoulder-high from the field.

I choose the match for its high drama and for the sportsmanship of the Welsh crowd in its acknowledgement of the brilliance of a great player, even though it brought about the defeat of their own country.

R. D. (Danny) Hearn

(Bedford & England)
6 caps for England (1966-67) as a centre.
Now based at Haileybury, Hertford.

MOST MEMORABLE 'TRY' WITNESSED
Oxford University (19) v Cambridge University (6), Twickenham, 8.12.1964

In the tenth minute of this Varsity match occurred the crucial incident of 'the try that wasn't'. From a line-out on the left Oxford, who had begun with the frustration of four successive Varsity match defeats boiling up inside them, moved the ball right and with an overlap created by blind-side wing A. K. Morgan, Rudd crossed in the south-east corner. Pandemonium!

The referee was walking back along the line of the touchdown when the Cambridge players drew his attention to their touch judge, J. R. H. Greenwood, standing motionless before that huge crowd with his flag up — and despite all the frenzy he never moved a muscle. So another throw-in followed; no try to Oxford but a real fright for Cambridge from which they hardly seemed to recover.

I choose this 'try' not only because it was my first really big game but also because never had an Oxford team gone into a game as such underdogs. With a superior record and three current internationals in their midfield (Mike Gibson, Geoff Frankom and David Rosser) Cambridge were expected to slaughter us. But our final total included four tries and, far from recording a record five successive victories as they had expected, Cambridge failed to score a try for the first time for half a decade.

MOST MEMORABLE TRY WITNESSED
Wales (34) v England (21), Cardiff, 15.4.1967

My choice is Keith Jarrett's try — seen by me as an opposition player! Here was an 18-year-old boy, playing in his first international at full-back, a position to which be was unaccustomed. He succeeded with seven place kicks out of eight, mostly from the touch-line, and scored his try at a crucial moment when England were recovering well from a shaky start — in a flash he was round Keith Savage and Roger Hosen and on his way to the corner. He kicked the goal.

I choose this try because of the improbability of so young a player on his international debut having such a game. How wrong could one be!

(opposite)
The 'try that wasn't' in the 1964 Varsity match. In the top picture the linesman's flag is already up as the Oxford backs launch the move which ended (lower picture) with A. K. Morgan touching down in the corner.

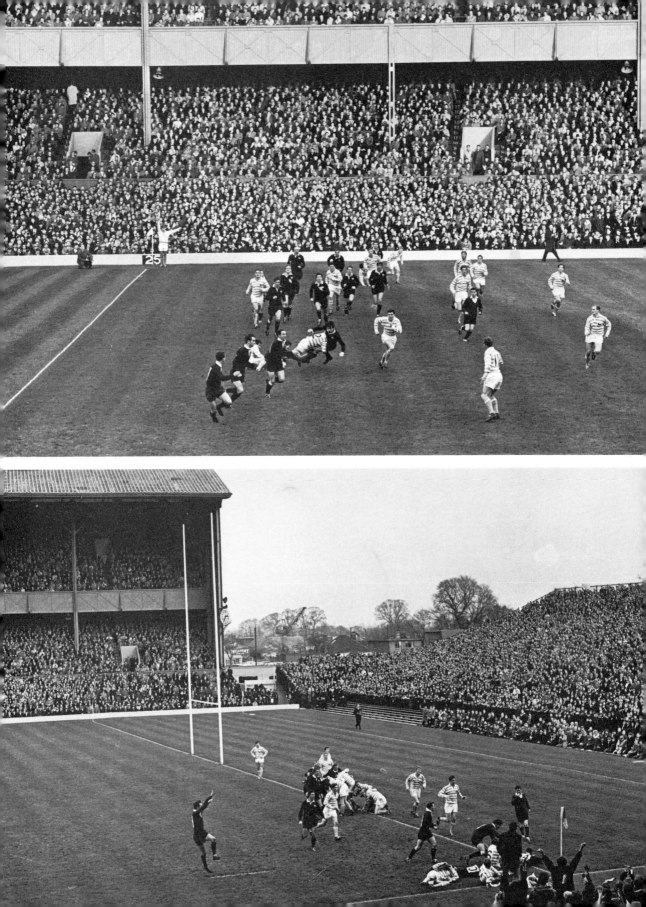

R. W. (Bob) Hiller

(Harlequins, England & British Isles)
19 caps for England (1968-72) as a full-back.
Now lives in London.

MOST MEMORABLE TRY SCORED
England (15) v Scotland (16), Twickenham, 20.3.1970

Since I did not score too many tries, one that inevitably sticks in the mind is that which Jeremy Janion initiated in this match. The burly Bedford centre made the early running, out of the England half down our left flank beneath the West Stand, before cutting sharply infield. Taylor and Wardlow took it on and I finally reached the right-hand corner flag beneath the East Stand.

Imaginatively conceived and in the end well executed, it was to be my only try for England.

MOST MEMORABLE TRIES WITNESSED
Hawke's Bay (6) v British Isles (25), Napier, 17.7.1971

Each of Gerald Davies's four tries that day, it seemed to me, showed different facets of his great skill and penetrative powers. What is more, they were all scored to the accompaniment of a deathly silence!

Jeremy Janion starts the move which culminated in Bob Hiller scoring a rare try – for England against Scotland in 1971.

Cyril B. Holmes
(Manchester & England)
3 caps for England (1947-48) as a wing.
Now lives in Bolton, Lancashire.

MOST MEMORABLE TRY SCORED
Lancashire & Cheshire (9) v Australians (8), Manchester, 26.11.1947

Just outside our 25 I intercepted a pass from the Wallabies' scrum-half to his wing, only to be checked by the wing-forward and number eight. Having shaken them off and forged ahead I was confronted by the full-back who was intent on tackling me into touch, but my speed proved too much for him. The final defender to beat was Trevor Allan — later to play Rugby League — who had come hurtling across from his midfield position, and there now followed a short, sharp race for the line. He only just failed to make up the necessary few yards between us, hitting me as I was in the act of grounding the ball. I spent half an hour on the table afterwards having bits of the Belle Vue dirt track extracted from my skin.

I choose this try because, for me, it was a highlight of 1947 — and 1947 was the year when I made the England side after many reserve tickets in the 1938-39 season.

Terry Holmes
(Cardiff, Wales & British Isles)
20 caps for Wales (1978-84, 1 Test for British Isles (1983) as a scrum-half.
Now lives in Cardiff.

MOST MEMORABLE PARTICIPATION IN TRY
Wales/England (37) v Scotland/Ireland (33), Cardiff, 29.11.1980

In injury time at the end of the game Scotland/Ireland led 33-31 and were given a scrum a few metres from the Wales/England line. John Robbie put the ball in, but when it came out awkwardly I was able to steal it from him, sprint away to our ten-metre line and kick ahead. The ball bounced badly for Andy Irvine and John Carleton was able to gather. When he was tackled, Mike Rafter won possession and fed me. After a few paces I gave to Gareth Davies on the burst, and he just reached the posts.

I choose this try because it covered the length of the field and involved several players. Good Rugby skills were included and it gave us victory in the dying seconds of a thoroughly enjoyable match seen by the Queen.

MOST MEMORABLE TRY WITNESSED
Scotland (9) v Wales (18), Murrayfield, 19.3.1977

I choose Phil Bennett's try because it had everything that is good in the Rugby game: daring, flair, support, continuity, timing and pace.

A. R. (Andy) Irvine

(Heriot's FP & Scotland)
51 caps for Scotland (1972-82), 9 Tests for British Isles (1974-80) as a full-back and wing.
Now lives in Edinburgh.

MOST MEMORABLE TRY SCORED
Wales/England (37) v Scotland/Ireland (33), Cardiff, 29.11.1980

Tony Ward picked up a loose ball in our 22 and passed to me. I began a counter-attack and linked with David Irwin and David Johnston. Back came the ball and I ended up scoring to round off a 75-metre move.

I choose this try because there was a great distance between the initiation of the move and the eventual try. It was one of those daring and immensely enjoyable counter-attacking tries that are attempted all too seldom.

MOST MEMORABLE TRY WITNESSED
Scotland (9) v Wales (18), Murrayfield, 19.3.1977

Phil Bennett's match-winning try for the opposition was, unfortunately, started by me when I chipped the ball over Wales's first-line defence for JPR (who else?) to fall and scoop it away. Steve Fenwick, Gerald Davies, Fenwick again and David Burcher were then instrumental in getting it to Phil Bennett who rounded the move off by jinking past Ian McLauchlan and sprinting to the posts. A truly great counter-attack, worthy of winning any match.

Phil Bennett ponders on the try he has just scored for Wales against Scotland in 1977. Andy Irvine was just one of several players to rate it the best he had ever witnessed.

David Irwin

(Queen's University, Belfast, Instonians, Ireland & British Isles)
16 caps for Ireland (1980-84), 3 Tests for British Isles (1983) as a centre.
Now lives in Belfast.

MOST MEMORABLE TRY SCORED
Ireland (21) v Wales (7), Dublin, 15.3.1980

An Irish back move broke down in front of the Welsh posts some 20 metres out. Our forwards won the ensuing ruck. Scrum-half Colin Patterson fed Paul McNaughton who swerved diagonally outwards towards the right corner flag. He and I brought off a perfect scissors move which left me a run of 15 metres to score.

I have two reasons for choosing this try. It came in my first game at home in front of the Dublin crowd. Also, it was the first try of the match and set Ireland off towards their biggest-ever win over Wales.

MOST MEMORABLE PARTICIPATION IN TRY
Wales/England (37) v Scotland/Ireland (33), Cardiff, 29.11.1980

Scotland/Ireland halted a Wales/England attack deep in their 22 before Andy Irvine got possession and decided to run out of defence. Although I was involved in the movement I also had a detached view of most of its magnificent progress. The ball went from Irvine to Irwin to Johnston and back to Irvine — who scored.

This illustrated the classic dictum that attack is the best form of defence. In this case it was superbly demonstrated by one of the world's best-ever attacking full-backs.

David Irwin of Ireland in action in the 1983 game against Wales in which he scored a try following a perfect scissors movement. It was his first in front of the Dublin crowd.

47

Peter Jackson

(Coventry, England & British Isles)
20 caps for England (1956-63), 5 Tests for British Isles (1959) as a wing.
Now lives at Castle Bromwich, Birmingham.

MOST MEMORABLE PARTICIPATION IN TRY
Wales (6) v England (13), Cardiff, 19.1.1963

With several new caps the England side was an unknown quantity. The ground and weather conditions were appalling. Braziers used to thaw the pitch made it a toss-up whether you needed spikes or skates. But the Cardiff Arms Park tension was there.

We had kept our line intact during early Welsh pressure, and Jim Roberts had twice thrown a long ball over the line-out enabling Richard Sharp to gain us valuable ground. To counter the ploy Wales's backs had come up to the advantage line in order to charge down the kicks. A gap was thus appearing which, in a quick-fire conversation with me, Malcolm Phillips said he hoped to exploit. Little did we realize how successful we would be!

After another long throw and a quick transfer by Mike Weston, Phillips runs at my opposite number Dewi Bebb. The Welsh centre D. B. Davies shouts to Bebb to leave Phillips to him and stay on me. But as I cut back for an inside pass, both defenders are taken out by Phillips — who, since he has not got the ball, cannot now be tackled and is free to run in a great arc to support me.

Wales's full-back Hodgson has angled me beautifully: there is no way through or around him. Apart from a kick ahead, seemingly risky because of the hard ground and unpredictability of the bounce, it is a question of waiting for Phillips to catch me up. This he does by sheer unadulterated pace, leaving me to take out Hodgson with what turns out to be a text-book pass!

From a prone position on the ground I can see Malcolm's legs giving out on him — but so are those of the cover defence!

Why this try? I have always felt that a true sportsman will raise himself above the conditions and adversity in its many aspects, and this was one of the few occasions when I had the pleasure of proving it. Apart from which, when you do everything right you have that marvellous inner satisfaction.

MOST MEMORABLE TRY WITNESSED
Warwickshire (8) v Lancashire (6), Coventry, 16.3.1964

Time was running out in this County Final with the score 6-5 to Lancashire. My chances of being the first captain to lead a side to the County title in three successive seasons seemed slim.

Then George Cole placed a kick almost onto the opposing corner flag. From the line-out and maul which ensued, a set scrum was ordered. Cole put the ball in, the pack shoved and strained, and over the line they went with the ball, but the referee — a Mr Luff — blew his whistle and called for another scrum. The tension was almost unbelievable.

Down went the packs again. In went the ball. For a second time our forwards pushed the opposition over the line — only for the referee to bring the sides back. Time by now seemed to be right against us; but as one of the players was having the magic sponge applied the dour, uncompromising voice of Phil Judd was heard: 'Right, lads, let's heave them onto the bank this time.' And they did so.

Because of weather conditions and the speed of the opposition the match had been particularly gruelling. To have claimed a pushover try thus says a lot for the courage and tenacity of the Warwickshire pack. To me their achievement epitomized the quality of the game's unsung heroes.

T. G. H. Jackson
(The Army & Scotland)
12 caps for Scotland (1947-49) as a wing.
Now lives at Kislingbury, Northamptonshire.

MOST MEMORABLE TRY SCORED
Richmond (3) v London Scottish (24), Richmond Athletic Ground, 15.11.1947

'He dribbled from half-way, beating man after man, before picking up to score', say my cuttings.

They are wrong in one respect. In fact, the ball bounced up into my hands!

I choose the try because of the unusual way in which I scored it and because of the considerable distance covered with a controlled dribble.

R. E. G. (Dickie) Jeeps
(Northampton, England & British Isles)
24 caps for England (1956-62), 13 Tests for British Isles (1955-62) as a scrum-half.
Latterly chairman of the Sports Council, Woburn Place, London.

MOST MEMORABLE PARTICIPATION IN TRY
South Africa (22) v British Isles (23), Johannesburg, 6.8.1955

Shortly after half-time in the First Test of the 1955 series the Lions were trailing 11-8 and, in days before replacements were allowed, had lost flanker Reg Higgins with a twisted knee. Then, after our seven forwards had won a strike against the head, Cliff Morgan at stand-off half called for a 'flat' pass from me, took the ball going very wide around Basie van Wyk, waggled his hips to get clear of the flanker's outstretched arm, and scorched in under the posts after a 20-yard dash — brilliant! The conversion gave us a lead which we held until the end.

MOST MEMORABLE TRY WITNESSED
England (9) v Australia (6), Twickenham, 1.2.1958

Behind at half-time, England were struggling against tourists who had already lost two Tests and were determined to end the sequence. Our centre Jeff Butterfield had been placed injured on a stretcher, only to abandon it and play on in a dazed condition — again in days before players could be replaced. We were, however, given hope by Eric Evans's fantastic half-time talk: 'If we win, we'll have a bloody good party tonight! Maybe! Maybe! Maybe!'

Late in the game our wing Peter Jackson received the ball on the right wing and, beating man after man with his side-step (not his pace!), scored in the corner to win the match for England.

This great try is a reminder that in those days England wings — men like Jackson, Peter Thompson and Jim Roberts — not only received the ball but also scored most of the tries. If you don't believe me, look at the records!

Barry John

(Llanelli, Cardiff, Wales & British Isles)
25 caps for Wales (1966-72), 5 Tests for the British Isles (1968-71) as a stand-off half.
Now lives in Radyr, South Glamorgan.

The elusive Barry John – his try for the Lions against New Zealand Universities in 1971 was a brilliant example of intuitive, 'sub-conscious' Rugby.

MOST MEMORABLE TRY SCORED
New Zealand Universities (6) v British Isles (27), Wellington, 6.7.1971

The night before this match Ray McLoughlin, our prop, Carwyn James, our coach, and myself were talking in the Lions' hotel. Carwyn was in the sort of mood when he could — and would, with great conviction — describe the Rugby which is played at a sub-conscious level as well as the conscious, Rugby which is intuitive and in which thinking plays little part. Ray on the other hand, a deep thinker who viewed everything objectively, could not grasp Carwyn's more metaphysical — for want of a better term — approach. He was still unconvinced of its validity when our discussion broke up.

The try I scored the following day was from 20 yards out and owed much to my feint to drop for goal. Thereafter the students never seemed to be on balance and I went past a number of them on my way to the posts. Everything seemed to have fallen into place: the players were in the positions I wanted them to be, and there was a sense of déjà vu as if I could see where a defender would go before he went there. It was so clear — as it the game had already been played in another time, another place.

In the stand Ray, a few seats from Carwyn, looked over and gave him the nod to acknowledge that now perhaps he did understand.

MOST MEMORABLE TRY WITNESSED
South Africa (25) v British Isles (20), Pretoria, 8.6.1968

I had dislocated a shoulder and was in an ambulance on the way to hospital. But I had already seen what Frik du Preez was capable of and when I heard his try described by the radio commentator could imagine vividly how he had done it.

Nevertheless, when I saw it later on film, it still took my breath away. Du Preez's sheer speed made everyone else appear to be standing still. He came around the front of the line-out, ran up the touch-line and side-stepped Tom Kiernan before crossing the Lions' goal-line.

This was a remarkable try for anyone to score, let alone a lock-forward. But Frik's indecent turn of speed, plus the ability to side-step, made him something different from any other forward I have seen. The incident taught me one very important lesson — never to underestimate any man's potential.

Cliff Jones
(Cambridge University, Cardiff & Wales)
13 caps for Wales (1934-38) as a stand-off half.
Now lives in Cowbridge, Mid Glamorgan.

MOST MEMORABLE TRY WITNESSED
Wales (34) v England (21), Cardiff, 15.4.1967

Besides kicking immaculately Keith Jarrett scored a marvellous try, throwing caution to the wind with the abandon of youth. An England touch-finder failed to make the distance and the Welsh full-back swooped in to take the high bounce, straighten up and race along the north touch-line for a try when he then converted.

To me his feat signalled the start of a golden era, when bold calculated risks were taken. At the time I was chairman of selection and the choice of Jarrett, a club centre with Newport, at full-back was a huge gamble. The Black and Ambers, in order to give assistance to the cause as it were, picked him in that position for a local derby against Newbridge before the England game — only to switch him back to centre at half-time! But in the international the experiment paid off beyond anyone's expectation.

D. Ken Jones
(Llanelli, Cardiff, Wales & British Isles)
14 caps for Wales (1962-66), 6 Tests for the British Isles (1962-66) as a centre.
Now lives in Cardiff.

MOST MEMORABLE TRY SCORED
South Africa (3) v British Isles (3), Johannesburg, 23.6.1962

With ten minutes left the British Isles were trailing 3-0. Our forwards won a line-out in our half and Gordon Waddell gave me a well-timed pass which I took on the burst to get past the Springbok midfield defenders. Then I had a lot of time in which to think — not always an advantage in sport! — before coming up to full-back Lionel Wilson whose aim was to channel me towards touch. Doug Hopwood, the South African number eight, was covering hard on the inside, but I risked coming off my right foot and had enough speed to reach the line.

The try was significant because, had we lost this first Test, South Africa might have raced away with the series. My memory of the game is vivid because it was my first Test abroad, and at the famous Ellis Park of all places.

MOST MEMORABLE TRY WITNESSED
South Africa (34) v British Isles (14), Bloemfontein, 25.8.1962

Mannetjies Roux's try showed all his virtues. Not a big man, but solidly built, he was very quick and possessed a devastating side step and swerve.

In Britain his reputation is less than shining because people remember the incident of Richard Sharp's broken jaw in the game before the first Test. In Britain two years earlier Roux had been involved in similar controversies, mainly surrounding alleged late tackles. This try against the Lions restored the balance.

John MacG. K. Kendall-Carpenter

(Oxford University, Bath & England)
25 caps for England (1949-54) as lock and
back-row forward.
Now headmaster of Wellington School, Somerset.

MOST MEMORABLE TRY SCORED
Scotland (3) v England (19), Murrayfield, 15.3.1952

England centre Brian Boobbyer cut through
near half-way and, when checked, passed to
Don White. With his path blocked on the
25-yard line the open-side wing forward handed on to me. Outflanking the cover and wrong-
footing the defending backs I was able to run
straight and score close to the posts. This was
the final try in England's comfortable win.

A few yards away, as it happened, was a film
camera and for the next 20 years until
Gaumont-British disappeared off the cinema
screen my try featured in the introductory
montage to the newsreel — and was thus seen by
more eyes than any other hitherto.

MOST MEMORABLE TRY WITNESSED
Wales (34) v England (21), Cardiff Arms Park, 15.4.1967

This was Keith Jarrett's match, the 18-year-old
— straight from school — scoring 19 points in a
splendid Welsh victory. His try, memorable in
itself, is an apt summary of the match when put
into context.

Two minutes earlier a high kick from David
Watkins had been aimed towards touch on the
north side of the ground. It fell short to the
experienced England full-back Roger Hosen
who, watching the ball carefully, allowed it to
bounce, collected it with his cricketer's hands
and, after steadying himself, found a reasonable
touch.

Then it was Keith Jarrett's turn. Colin
McFadyean put in a diagonal kick which failed
to find touch. Jarrett, some distance away at full
back and faced with the prospect of taking the
ball on the full or on the bounce, raced forward
to collect it in his stride, outflanked the England
defenders and with unstoppable momentum
sprinted on for a brilliant try.

These two pieces of play epitomized the
difference between the two sides in a remarkable, high-scoring game. It was a triumph for
youth over experience — the one playing it safe,
the other with that glorious spirit of enterprise,
born of high hopes and young adventure, which
proved sufficient all on its own to deny England
the Triple Crown and a share of the Championship title.

Basil Kenyon
(Border & South Africa)
1 Test for South Africa (1949) as a flanker.
Now lives in Witelsbos, South Africa.

Ian Kirkpatrick
(Canterbury, Poverty Bay & New Zealand)
39 Tests for New Zealand (1967-77) as a flanker.
Now lives in Gisborne, New Zealand.

MOST MEMORABLE TRY SCORED
Border (9) v New Zealand (0), Border, 15.6.1949

I won the toss and decided to play against a strong wind. At half-time the score was 0-0 and I knew that, with the wind, we had a good chance of winning.

In the sixth minute of the second half we had the put-in at a scrum just outside the All Blacks' 25. I told Okker Woodward our scrum-half to break and look for my support on the inside. He did as suggested, slipped the ball to me, and I beat off two tackles for a try which I touched down in a concussed state.

I choose it because in this fourth game of their tour it was the first conceded by the New Zealanders.

MOST MEMORABLE TRY WITNESSED
France (3) v South Africa (25), Paris, 16.2.1952

From a scrum near the right touch-line on South Africa's 25 the ball flashed from Fonnie du Toit along our back-line via Hansie Brewis, Tjol Lategan and Ryk van Schoor to 'Chum' Ochse who got around his man and passed back inside. The forwards gained ground with short, snappy passes before giving possession again to the backs. Things had happened so quickly that Ochse was not in position when the ball came back his way, but Paul Johnstone had crossed from the opposite wing to take a pass and link again with the pack. Away they went again, back came the ball again at the right moment — and this time Chum was there. When cut off he put in a short cross-kick which Basie van Wyk, with the other seven forwards all at hand, gathered to dive in and score.

I choose this try as a great one to end an outstanding match and crown a great tour. How often the ball was handled no one will ever know now. What is known is that Johnny Buchler, the Springbok full-back, was the only South African not to handle.

MOST MEMORABLE TRY SCORED
New Zealand (22) v British Isles (12), Christchurch, 10.7.1971

After a line-out won by New Zealand close to half-way, play moved infield with the All Black forwards mauling for possession. The ball ended up with me, and somehow I found myself clear on the Lions' side of the maul with a big gap ahead. I just ran as hard as I could in the direction of the corner flag. The tacklers, who challenged from both sides, came from slightly behind, which made it easier to fend them off. I

Ian Kirkpatrick – scorer of a driving, hard-running try against the 1971 British Lions in Christchurch, New Zealand.

was mighty relieved to reach the goal-line!

I choose this try because I guess it was one of my better ones — and because it has been shown on TV on numerous occasions, which makes it easier to remember and describe.

MOST MEMORABLE PARTICIPATION IN TRY
South Africa (20) v New Zealand (17), Johannesburg, 12.9.1970

Bryan Williams's try in this game began at a scrum midway between the South African 25 and half-way where our hooker Urlich won the ball. Sid Going broke on the short side for several yards and gave a superbly timed pass to BG who beat his opposite number near the corner flag and proceeded to head for the posts. He side-stepped two defenders in the in-goal area before scoring a great try under the bar.

This try often comes to mind — mainly, I guess, because of the confidence Bryan Williams showed in beating two opponents behind the goal-line.

Roy Laidlaw
(Jedforest, Scotland & British Isles)
28 caps for Scotland (1980-84), 4 Tests for British Isles (1983) as a scrum-half.
Now lives in Jedburgh, Borders.

MOST MEMORABLE TRIES SCORED
Scotland (13) v Ireland (15), Murrayfield, 15.1.1983

This try was Scotland's only one, and came from a long solo break in which I left a number of defenders in my wake.

Though scored for a losing Scottish team it remains my favourite because it was my first at international level.

Ireland (9) v Scotland (32), Dublin, 3.3.1984

After four or five minutes Scotland won an important line-out through Campbell, the forwards drove on, and the ball came back to me from the ruck. I decided to go on my own, checked to tie in the opposition back row, sold a dummy, straightened up, and just reached the line.

I choose this try because it launched Scotland on course for a Triple Crown, our first since 1938. After a quarter of an hour we were 14-0 up and the match was as good as won.

Roy Laidlaw scored a try which launched Scotland on their course to the Triple Crown in 1984.

Mark Loane
(Queensland & Australia)
28 Tests for Australia (1973-82) as a number eight.
Now lives in Brisbane, Australia.

MOST MEMORABLE TRY SCORED
Queensland (18) v Scotland (7), Brisbane, 13.6.1982

I went in for this try from some 30 metres. It was particularly memorable to me because I had played in several Queensland teams which had narrowly failed to beat touring sides — and had missed the great win over New Zealand in 1980. Against Scotland my try put us in front and we ran out winners. This was my last game for Queensland against a touring side, and it was a nice note to go out on.

MOST MEMORABLE PARTICIPATION IN TRIES
New Zealand (16) v Australia (30), Auckland, 9.9.1978

Not one try — but the four scored by Greg Cornelsen in a Test when Australia achieved a record score against the All Blacks. The build-up and finish to all four were superb.

Colin McFadyean
(Moseley, England & British Isles)
11 caps for England (1966-68), 4 Tests for British Isles (1966) as a centre.
Now lives at West Wickham, Kent.

MOST MEMORABLE TRY SCORED
Ireland (3) v England (8), Dublin, 11.2.1967

Well beaten in all the set pieces, we had spent most of the game defending desperately against the sallies of Gibson, O'Leary, McBridge, Murphy and Goodall. When Peter Glover was injured, I had been moved to the wing, a position I didn't like much. Now, with a few minutes left, it was 3-3 — a penalty to each side.

Ireland won possession around half-way and started to run, only for the ball to go loose after a hard tackle on Jerry Walsh. I got a foot to it and as it was rolling end-over-end I knew it would pop up. It did, some 30 metres out, allowing me to take it in full stride. I swerved away from the noise and curved back under the posts. Roger Hosen converted and we won the match.

I choose this try because it bore no relation to the game as it had been played. Even in the dressing room we sat in stunned, exhausted silence. No one in the England team could credit that we had won, no one in the Irish team could believe that they had lost!

MOST MEMORABLE TRY WITNESSED
Wales (34) v England (21), Cardiff, 15.4.1967

The Jarrett try. Under pressure near England's 25 and going open, I kicked high and wide, not a bad percentage kick. The ball landed on its point and sat up. Keith Savage nearly got hold of it, with a clear 50-yard run to the line before him. Instead Keith Jarrett, coming from God knows where, took it and outstripped our cover for a stunning try at the other end.

Even at the time it was unreal: several of Jarrett's place kicks swerved between the posts as the massed Welsh crowd blew in unison; Gerald Davies scored two tries that no one can remember; England scored four tries at Cardiff and lost; a lock, Barton, got two of them; this was the only game Wales won that season — England had been on for the Triple Crown.

Ian McGeechan
(Headingley, Scotland & British Isles)
32 caps for Scotland (1972-79), 8 Tests for the British Isles (1974-77) as a centre.
Now lives in Leeds, West Yorkshire.

MOST MEMORABLE TRY SCORED
North Auckland (7) v British Isles (18), Whangerei, 6.8.1977

This game took place at a stage in the tour when our forwards had lost a little confidence in the backs. The day was wet and blustery and the Lions were trying to assert themselves.

As I took a pass from Phil Bennett we seemed to be going nowhere yet again. I decided to throw caution to the winds and take on my opposite number, an All Black centre. Beating him set me off on a jinking run which took me past the back row and Sid Going and eventually round the full-back to score near the posts. The resultant six points decided the game for us.

The try was important for me because I had to make it, and in so doing recovered the confidence and assertiveness which I had lost. In three-quarter play going for a break represents a mental barrier which seems hard to crack when one has doubts.

MOST MEMORABLE PARTICIPATION IN TRY
Scotland (10) v Wales (9), Murrayfield, 3.2.1973

Billy Steele's try lifted us to a 10-0 lead after 20 minutes and made possible one of the rare wins recorded by Scotland over Wales in a succession of exciting matches between the two nations in the early seventies.

Billy ('the dancer') was an underrated player, but with this try he really showed his mettle, beating such rugged tacklers as Mervyn Davies and J. P. R. Williams in a very small space. It made me aware of the match-winning qualities of great wings like Steele and Gerald Davies who could guarantee to beat at least the first man, thereby causing untold panic in defences.

I choose the try because it occurred early in my international career when I could still hardly credit that I was playing with and against some of world Rugby's great men. In this game I 'came of age' as an international player.

Ian McLauchlan
(Jordanhill, Scotland & British Isles)
43 caps for Scotland (1969-79), 8 Tests for British Isles (1971-74 as a prop-forward.
Now lives in Edinburgh.

MOST MEMORABLE TRY SCORED
New Zealand (3) v British Isles (9), Dunedin, 26.6.1971

John Bevan, the British Isles wing, attacked but lost the ball. New Zealand's scrum-half, Sid Going, picked up and fed Alan Sutherland who kicked for touch. I charged the kick down, the ball rebounded across the goal-line, and I fell on it.

I choose this try because I did not score too often at top level. Furthermore, this was a try which set the Lions on a game-winning and series-winning run over New Zealand.

MOST MEMORABLE PARTICIPATION IN TRY
Scotland (22) v England (12), Murrayfield, 21.1.1976

An England kick-ahead was fielded inside our 22 by Scotland wing David Shedden. He beat the approaching Englishmen and opened up to Mike Biggar, Sandy Carmichael and Alan Lawson who sprinted the last 20 metres to score near the posts.

The try symbolized all that is good in Rugby, sweeping the whole length of the field and involving forwards and backs. Alan Lawson later scored a second try.

Hugh McLeod

(Hawick, Scotland & British Isles)
40 caps for Scotland (1954-62), 6 Tests for British Isles (1959) as a prop-forward.
Now lives at Hawick, Borders.

MOST MEMORABLE PARTICIPATION IN TRIES
Ireland (6) v Scotland (20), Dublin, 24.2.1962

From what was described in those days as a loose maul, Scotland's scrum-half Stan Coughtrie burst up our right and interpassed with his partner Gordon Waddell. I found myself well positioned to accept a pass from the stand-off before sending Arthur Smith in at the corner — a snappy move in which only four Scots were involved though six passes were taken and given. Scotland had been leading a wee bit precariously 12-6 and that try with Ken Scotland's conversion put us in the clear. I am not quite sure how I got into the linking position but I kid myself that, 20 years ahead of my time, I was cleverly 'standing off' through brilliant anticipation.

I choose the try because it actually ensured that, having beaten Wales 8-3, we were two-thirds of the way to a Triple Crown (only for a 3-3 draw with England to thwart that ambition). Also, it was a real pleasure for a bow-legged prop-forward to give a scoring pass to one of Scotland's great wings!

Our handsome win also stays in my memory because it was my 39th international and my last away from home. After the England game I hung up my boots.

New Zealand (6) v British Isles (9), Auckland, 19.9.1959

This was the last Test in the 1959 series. The Lions had lost the first three (though only in the third were the All Blacks clearly the better side). Now, at Auckland, we had scored two tries but Don Clark had put over two penalties for New Zealand so that it was 6-6 with just 15 minutes to go.

Then, from a scrummage some 35 yards out from the All Blacks' line, Andy Mulligan went right before giving a delicious little reverse pass to his partner Bev Risman. The latter took off to the left, then brilliantly side-stepped wing B. E. McPhail, veered out beyond scrum-half Urbahn, and stayed just in front of flanker Pickering before beating Clark's tackle with a scoring dive to the corner flag.

The try was memorable because it brought a rare win for the Lions. All New Zealand said we deserved it — and you have to play well to get that kind of praise Down Under! I had played in all six Tests on tour — two against Australia and four in New Zealand — and can still feel the sheer joy and pride of being a member of a winning Test team against the All Blacks. Incidentally, in that series the British Isles scored nine tries against only seven by New Zealand.

Murray Mexted

(Wellington & New Zealand)

20 Tests for New Zealand (1979-83) as a number eight.

Now lives in Wellington, New Zealand.

MOST MEMORABLE TRY SCORED
Scotland (6) v New Zealand (20), Murrayfield, 10.11.1979

It was New Zealand's ball at a short line-out midway between Scotland's 22 and the half-way line. Andy Haden having drawn David Gray out of contention, Andy Dalton threw to me running forward ahead of my opposite number Lambie, a ploy which also enabled me to get past the Scottish scrum-half Lawson. Next I beat off the challenges of Milne and McLauchlan who had withdrawn from the line-out. By now I was up to full speed and was able to step inside Hay and Irvine to reach the line.

The try is memorable to me because this game was my maiden appearance in a full New Zealand Test side.

MOST MEMORABLE TRY WITNESSED
New Zealand (22) v British Isles (12), Christchurch, 10.7.1971

In this game Ian Kirkpatrick's try was the best solo score I have ever watched. Against the world's best at that time he showed strength, speed, individual flair and incredible determination.

Murray Mexted in action in the Scotland v. All Blacks game at Murrayfield in 1979. It was his first full international, and he crowned his performance with a try-scoring run through the Scottish defence.

Syd Millar

(Ballymena, Ireland & British Isles)
37 caps for Ireland (1958-70), 9 Tests for British Isles (1959-68) as a prop.
Now lives in Ballymena, Northern Ireland.

MOST MEMORABLE TRY WITNESSED
South African Invitation XV (19) v British Isles (22), Potchefstroom, 21.5.1980

The British Isles were behind with minutes to go, and both teams were tired after a bruising game. The Invitation XV were camped on the Lions' 22 and seemingly holding an unbreakable stranglehold, conscious of the effect a win would have on their personal ambitions and roared on by a partisan crowd. I myself, as touring manager, was aware that the Lions could be set to lose a first game outside Tests in South Africa since 1962. But drama was about to unfold.

At a line-out on the Lions' 22 John O'Driscoll leapt high and palmed to scrum-half Colin Patterson, who sent a quick pass to stand-off half David Richards. He took it flat, straightened, and found O'Driscoll up inside him. The flanker made a few yards, handed on to Gareth Williams, who passed to Derek Quinnell, who was stopped but managed to give Patterson the ball. On it went to Richards, who missed out Clive Woodward to give Mike Slemen a chance. Bruce Hay came up inside Slemen from full-back, took the pass, but was tackled.

The Lions' forwards won the ruck speedily: again it was Patterson to Richards to Quinnell, and now Jim Renwick and Elgan Rees took up the running. The latter cut infield, was caught on the South African 22 — there again was Quinnell to rescue the ball and give to Patterson. He went left, short-passed to Richards who gave to Woodward who was tackled; the ball ran loose. Slemen picked up, sent infield to Williams, but he was tackled, and again the ball ran loose. In despair a South African boot hacked the ball upfield and as the Invitation XV streamed out of defence they must have felt relief that the danger had seemingly been averted, for only Renwick was back for the Lions.

But Richards was ahead of the throng; he flipped the ball up to Renwick who had no support and seemed bound to kick — but he ran, jinking to make room and finding Alan Phillips to his right (with some pace for a hooker). Again Patterson was put in possession, and again Rees on the right wing. He stepped inside, accelerated, but was caught on the opposition 22. Another ruck was won quickly: Patterson to Richards, to Renwick, to Woodward, to Hay coming up from full-back again. He crashed a tackle. Slemen had sensed the situation; he moved inside, took Hay's pass, jinked and ran diagonally — and scored from half-way out!

The South African players were on their knees — the crowd were on their feet enjoying the sheer delight of it all, clapping and cheering as if the home team had scored the try. To see the ball in play for such a period — one minute, 36 seconds — and pass through 33 pairs of hands was more than most of them had ever witnessed before. Magic!

I always associate Derek Quinnell more than anyone else with that try as, in addition to supporting and handling, he also won the vital balls, on one occasion seeming to ruck the whole South African pack on his own. However, it was also a tremendous team effort demonstrating the great character of a side whose toll of injuries was far above that of any other touring party. It is also worth emphasizing that the try emerged from a pressure situation.

Cliff Morgan

(Cardiff, Wales & British Isles)
29 caps for Wales (1951-58), 4 Tests for British Isles (1955) as a stand-off half.
Now lives in London.

MOST MEMORABLE PARTICIPATION IN TRY
England (6) v Wales (8), Twickenham, 19.1.1952

In the words of Max Boyce, 'I was there!' Wales had been given little chance of beating England but in the end Ken Jones's two tries did it for us. The second was a classic three-quarter move when Lewis Jones, nursing a pulled muscle, limped into the line to make a gap. But it is the first of Ken's tries that lives on in my memory.

The Welsh pack, in storming form, were giving their backs a decent supply of the ball. At a line-out on our 25 Roy John reared, collected and fed Rex Willis. Seeing Don White, the England wing-forward, bearing down on me Rex took a couple of steps and passed the ball to me behind White's back. I remember stepping inside 'Nim' Hall and then back towards the middle of the field. After 30 yards or so there was a red jersey alongside. As Ken and I approached England's full-back, Bill Hook, we did a scissors and Ken ran 50 yards at Olympic speed to score a try between the posts.

I choose this try because a wing in full flight is one of the rare joys of Rugby football.

MOST MEMORABLE TRY WITNESSED
Combined Transvaal (18) v Barbarians (16), Johannesburg, 24.5.1958

This match, containing many brilliant attacking moves, concluded a tour of unforgettable thrills. After it the question was asked, 'Did a Press photographer rob the Barbarians of a draw?' The unfortunate cameraman, lingering behind the goal-line, threw himself down to avoid the speeding Tony O'Reilly — too late, for although Tony hurdled him he tripped and fell. So instead of an easy kick in front of the Transvaal posts our conversion attempt had to be taken where O'Reilly went down, way out near the corner flag.

I select this try for three reasons: first, the Barbarian pack won glorious possession; secondly, there followed a classic break by our scrum-half, Andrew Mulligan; and thirdly, with all the grace and pace of a remarkable wing, Tony O'Reilly showed his class.

Perhaps I should add one more thing: despite the fact that a photographer tripped him up, thus denying the Barbarians the chance of two match-saving points, there was never a word of complaint from the Irishman. But then — that was O'Reilly, a big and stylish man in every way.

Graham Mourie
(Taranaki & New Zealand)
21 Tests for New Zealand (1977-82) as a flanker. Now lives in Opunake, New Zealand.

MOST MEMORABLE TRY SCORED
Wales (3) v New Zealand (23), Cardiff, 1.11.1980

The try came after an intense period of pressure by New Zealand on the Welsh line. We attacked initially through Mexted from the back of a line-out on the All Black right and then down the blind-side where we had an overlap. Wales's centre David Richards intercepted, preventing a possible score, and was in turn run down by Nicky Allan when maybe he should have been able to go the length of the field. A ruck formed on half-way, at which we won the ball, moving it again on the same side of the field. Bruce Robertson made ground and passed to me about 25 metres out. With Ackerman confronting, I offered a wisp of a dummy to Stu Wilson on the scissors and scored at the corner.

I choose this try not only because it was a personal highlight but also because of its crucial effect on the way the game went. We had put a lot of pressure on the Welsh without being able to score (I realized afterwards that if Richards had got away for a try it could have changed the match), so mine was the blow which destroyed our opponents' morale and ensured a memorable victory.

Peope have often asked why I didn't give the ball to Wilson. My reply has always been that in our earlier game against Swansea the same movement had occurred with him taking my pass and scoring and we had agreed afterwards that next time it would be my turn!

The All Blacks captain Graham Mourie dives over in the corner to open the scoring in his side's 23-3 defeat of the Welsh in 1980.

W. A. (Bill) Mulcahy

(Bective Rangers, Ireland & British Isles
35 caps for Ireland (1958-65), 6 Tests for British
Isles (1958-65) as a lock-forward.
Now lives in Skerries, Co. Dublin.

MOST MEMORABLE PARTICIPATION IN TRY
England (5) v Ireland (18), Twickenham, 8.2.1964

A short distance from our own line and about
25 yards in from the right-hand touch-line
Ireland won a set scrum. The ball was sent
quickly by scrum-half Jimmy Kelly to Mike
Gibson at stand-off half who took the pass at full
stride and was away, knifing diagonally left-
wards through the defence. On the England
ten-yard line, with everybody chasing hard to
head him off, he gave a beautifully timed
reversed pass to centre Jerry Walsh cutting
from left to right. As Walsh raced down the
right hand touch-line wing P. J. Casey came in
and gratefully accepted a further reverse pass
from Walsh, which sent him on to the posts
unopposed.

By any standards this was a top-class try,
clearly depicting the genius of Gibson. We went
on to a big win, very gratifying to myself as
skipper that day.

MOST MEMORABLE TRY WITNESSED
Ireland (0) v England (6), Dublin, 9.2.1957

Ireland's left-wing threw to a line-out 25 yards
from his line. The ball came back awkwardly on
the Irish side. Under pressure the scrum-half
tried to clear over his forwards' heads but failed
to find touch. England's right-wing, Peter Jackson, fielded and set off down the right touch-
line. He stepped off his right foot and then,
without losing pace it seemed, off his left, and
then once more off his right to go screaming
through where no space looked available, to
score near the right corner.

This was a marvellous try for, on catching the
ball, Jackson seemed to react instantly and
instinctively. His several changes of direction off
either foot and without loss of pace took him
through the tightest of areas with hardly a
finger laid on him. A highly individual score,
displaying unique skill.

*P. J. Casey touches down for Ireland against England in 1964, a
try which owed much to the genius of Gibson.*

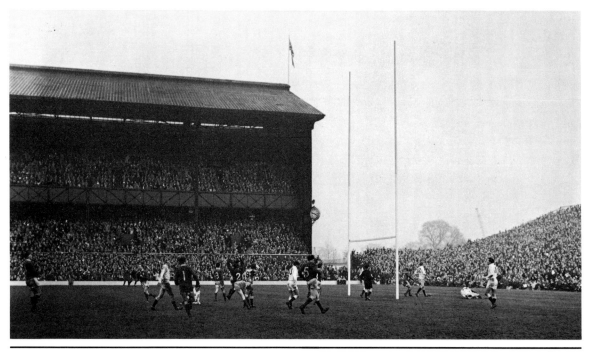

A. J. F. O'Reilly

(O. Belvedere, Leicester, Ireland & British Isles)
29 caps for Ireland (1955-70), 10 Tests for British
Isles (1955-59) as centre and wing.
Now lives in Pittsburgh, USA.

MOST MEMORABLE TRY SCORED
New Zealand (6) v British Isles (9), Auckland, 19.9.1959

That great Olympian Ken Jones had established
a record for players on tour in New Zealand of
16 tries with the 1950 Lions. I had equalled this
record three games from the end of our 1959
tour and if injury did not intervene had a
reasonable chance of beating it. However,
strange are the ways of this mysterious game
and seven minutes from the end of our last
match, the final Test, I had yet to score the
critical try. What is more the All Blacks were
leading 6-3.

The British Isles attacked down the blind side
through Andy Mulligan, our scrum-half, with
myself close at hand. The cover was drawn and
New Zealand's wing McPhail hesitated a vital
second. I took the pass, the line appeared, and
Don Clarke, McPhail and I plunged over the
line together as I scored that elusive try. I can
still feel the cold, muddy ball on my face as we
crashed to the ground.

Bev Risman won the game for us with a try of
rare brilliance three minutes later.

MOST MEMORABLE PARTICIPATION IN TRY
South Africa (22) v British Isles (23), Johannesburg, 6.8.1955

My second reminiscence would have been about
Risman's try had it not been for that scored by
Cliff Morgan in this game.

Though the catalyst of the 1955 Lions, Morgan nursed memories of a forbidding day in
1951 when, on his third appearance for Wales,
he faced South Africa's all-conquering back row
of Hennie Muller, Stephen Fry and the fear-
some Basie van Wyk, the Yul Brynner of world
flankers. It was a long, harrowing afternoon for
the multi-talented stand-off half. Wales lost, and
the experience remained vividly with Cliff over
the next four years.

On this day in 1955 the Springboks (with van
Wyk and Fry again in their back row) established an 11-8 lead. The British Isles then lost
flanker Reg Higgins and, this being in days
before replacements were allowed, had to play
the final 40 minutes at 6,000 feet with 14 men.
It was Morgan's magical pace on the outside
break which changed the course of the game.
Receiving the ball going left from just outside
the South African 25, he ran in an arc outside
the desperately grasping hands of van Wyk and
Ulyate, the Springbok scrum-half, to touch
down under the bar without a hand being laid
on him. Its brilliance is captured in the well-
known photograph — and its poignancy, for
van Wyk never played again for South Africa.

Keith Oxlee

(Natal & South Africa)
19 Tests for South Africa (1960-65) as stand-off half.
Now lives in Glenashley, South Africa.

MOST MEMORABLE TRY SCORED
South Africa (3) v New Zealand (11), Cape Town, 23.7.1960

The movement which led to my try started with a South African put-in at a set scrum just five metres from New Zealand's line. The Springboks heeled cleanly and our scrum-half Dick Lockyear ran wide, drawing the loose forwards. I came up on his inside to take a reverse pass and found a clear gap through which I went to score.

I choose the try because it was unique in my experience. At no stage had Dick and I practised the move which led to the score. We planned it in the bus on the way from our hotel to Newlands.

MOST MEMORABLE PARTICIPATION IN TRY
South Africa (34) v British Isles (14), Bloemfontein, 25.8.1962

The try in this Fourth Test by the Springbok centre Mannetjies Roux was by far the most exciting I have seen executed by one player. It was a wholly individual effort with no help from any team-mate.

South Africa were defending inside the 25 when Mannetjies received the ball. We all expected him to clear for touch, but he elected to run — and just kept on running for the Lions' line. In the course of it he left five defenders prone and gasping on the ground with side-steps and swerves that were outstanding. The final result was an unforgettable try 15 yards to the left of the posts. I know the distance as I was doing the place-kicking — and could never understand why Mannetjies did not run round between the posts!

Alun Pask

(Abertillery, Wales & British Isles)
26 caps for Wales (1961-67), 8 Tests for the British Isles (1962-66) as a number eight.
Now lives in Blackwood, Gwent.

MOST MEMORABLE TRY SCORED
Wales (28) v Fiji (22), Cardiff, 26.9.1964.

International Rugby in the early sixties was dour and Fiji, who had arrived in Wales as a completely unknown side, reminded us what it was all about — simply handling and running with the ball. The Test against Wales was unforgettable, containing non-stop action and 13 tries to thrill the 50,000 crowd basking in brilliant sunshine. The tourists came back from 28-9 down to score 13 points in the game's last quarter.

My try, one of seven by Wales, began from a Welsh heel at a midfield scrum just inside Fiji's half. I picked up and ran down the blind side with the ball held in my outstretched hand. Several opponents kept their eyes on it and not on my legs, thus finding it hard to judge a tackle, and I managed to weave and dummy my way past them almost as far as the goal-line. Here I was confronted by a very large Fijian, Tuisese; there was no way I could go round him so I lowered a shoulder and, at full speed, toppled him backwards. My timing must have been perfect for I can clearly remember feeling no impact. Then I dived across the line, the ball still outstretched in my hand.

At the dinner following this marvellous, never-to-be-forgotten game I asked one of the tourists what their tactics had been for the game. 'Tactics?' he asked in a bemused manner. 'No tactics — we just play Rugby.'

MOST MEMORABLE PARTICIPATION IN TRY
South Africa (3) v British Isles (3), Johannesburg, 23.6.1962

Ken Jones's try made a lasting impression on me for it was scored during my first Test for the British Isles on my first Lions tour. To play at Ellus Park was itself a tremendous thrill, though also a daunting experience before 75,000 spectators in whose eyes the Springboks were clear favourites.

Though the tourists caused a surprise by winning the forward battle, the Springboks went ahead with a try started by Ken Jones himself, a kick ahead delivering possession to our opponents for whom John Gainsford scored an unconverted try. But with only ten minutes left our centre made amends. Receiving the ball from Gordon Waddell just inside our own half, he went past the Springbok midfield men with tremendous acceleration and had a run of 55 yards to the line. Lionel Wilson, the South African full-back, came across to cut him off only to be beaten by a beautiful jink. Pursuers Doug Hopwood and Mannetjies Roux kept up the chase but with five yards to go Ken dived in for a great try.

It was a fantastic feeling to see Ken reach the line, but a pity that our skipper Arthur Smith could not convert the try and give the Lions victory. To win the first Test would have been a tremendous boost to our confidence which could well have sent us on to win the Test series.

Colin Patterson
(Instonians, Ireland & British Isles)
11 caps for Ireland (1978-80), 3 Tests for British Isles (1980) as a scrum-half.
Now lives in Donaghadee, Northern Ireland.

MOST MEMORABLE PARTICIPATION IN TRY
South African Invitation XV (19) v British Isles (22), Potchefstroom, 21.5.1980

The try, scored eventually by Mike Slemen, started at a line-out on our 22. David Richards, at stand-off half, broke up to the 10-metre line and fed the back row, who drove on upfield, The Lions handled, and the South African XV covered and tackled, for over a minute and a half.

The try won the game and the crowd's respect. Just before the line-out we had been pelted with tangerines and other fruit, but after the try spectators stood for a minute applauding.

MOST MEMORABLE TRY WITNESSED
Ireland (20) v Wales (12), Dublin, 23.1.1982

Irish stand-off half Ollie Campbell took the ball from his inside half Robbie McGrath at a scrum 10 metres from the Welsh line and 15 metres from the left-hand touch-line. He faked to go right and ran left instead. There followed three dummies before a perfect pass delivered to Moss Finn who ran in the try from two or three yards.

I choose the try because it climaxed a superb individual effort by Campbell against good opposition and started the Irish team on its way to a Triple Crown.

Malcolm Phillips
(Fylde & England)
25 caps for England (1958-64) as a centre.
Now lives in Bolton, Lancashire.

MOST MEMORABLE TRY SCORED
Wales (6) v England (13), Cardiff, 19.1.1963

In January 1963 Britain was gripped by arctic conditions. Unable to find a pitch suitable for our eve-of-the-month run-out, the England XV had used the beach at Porthcawl; and when the straw was lifted at Cardiff Arms Park before next day's kick-off the turf immediately froze.

Wales had the best of the opening quarter without taking their chances to build a lead, and it was England who got the first score. Left-wing Jim Roberts triggered it with a long throw over a line-out on our 25 which reached Mike Weston. He fed me and I scissored with my wing, the inimitable Peter Jackson, who drew the nearest Welsh defenders onto him like a magnet. Though normally he mesmerized the opposition before releasing the ball, on this occasion 'Jacko' gave a surprisingly quick return pass which put me in an outflanking position on half-way. Into the freezing wind it was a long haul to the Welsh line at the river end of the ground, but fortunately for me the defence was suffering as well and I was able to round off a move in which the ball must have travelled some hundred yards.

The try was particularly satisfying to me after two years out of the England side through loss of form and a shoulder-pinning operation. After my return to international football in this game, I went on to add 12 more caps to the 13 I already held.

Incidentally England won the game — at the time of writing still our last victory in the Principality, and a matter of very mixed feelings for me!

Steve Pokere
(Southland & New Zealand)
13 Tests for New Zealand (1981-83) as a centre.
Now lives at Invercargill, New Zealand.

MOST MEMORABLE TRY SCORED
New Zealand Maoris (66) v Spain (3), Madrid, 21.11.1982

From a Spanish kick-off I gathered the ball between the Maoris' 22- and 10-metre lines. The whole Spanish XV was naturally between me and their goal-line, but I threaded my way between them to score.

The try is memorable to me because of the number of players who had to be beaten to enable me to score. Also, it was my fourth (out of five) in the game.

MOST MEMORABLE TRY WITNESSED
Australia (9) v New Zealand (12), Brisbane, 28.6.1980

The ball was spun along the All Black back-line within their 22 to Bruce Robertson who beat a couple of men before passing to inside support players. The ball went through several New Zealanders' hands before Hika Reid scored at the posts.

I choose the try because there is no team against whom I enjoy seeing tries scored more than Australia! Another reason is that Bruce, who started it, was originally left out of the touring team. The try contributed considerably towards victory in the Test and the avoidance of an embarrassing white-wash in the series.

Brian Price

(Newport, Wales & British Isles)
32 caps for Wales (1961-69), 4 Tests for the British
Isles (1966) as a lock.
Now lives in Caldicot, Gwent.

MOST MEMORABLE PARTICIPATION IN TRY
Wales (24) v Ireland (11), Cardiff, 8.3.1969

Just before half-time we were awarded a penalty
on the Welsh left some 25 yards from the Irish
line. We needed points on the board in what
had been a bruising, difficult encounter in many
ways! I called up our place-kicker Keith Jarrett
but did not give the referee any indication that
he would aim at goal.

Neither did Keith. In the heat of this torrid
game, prompted by our prop Denzil Williams,
he showed the courage, presence of mind and
initiative to take a tapped penalty. The Irish did
not see it, for they had turned their backs. So
had I!

Then came the roar of the crowd. I turned to
look and saw the great bulk of Denzil thunder-
ing in for a try. Ireland had been resisting
tenaciously but this try sank them.

*Denzil Williams in action in the 1969 Wales v. Ireland game in
which he scored a thunderous try following a tapped penalty.*

Graham Price

(Pontypool, Wales & British Isles)
41 caps for Wales (1975-83), 8 Tests for the British Isles (1977-80) as a prop-forward.
Now lives in Pontypool, Gwent.

MOST MEMORABLE TRY SCORED
France (10) v Wales (25), Paris, 18.1.1975

In some ways I'm glad that the try I scored on my debut for Wales came at the end of our game at Parc des Princes. Had it come at the beginning I'd have been shattered for the rest of the match! To go some 70 yards after 79 minutes can be put down to will-power and the kind of fitness Ray Prosser demands at Pontypool.

It was a unique situation which I had never found myself in before and which never cropped up afterwards. A prop may run 40 yards against a bad team; but on the rare occasions when he scores against strong opponents it is usually from four or five yards' range with defenders hanging round his neck. Again, Barry Llewelyn and Glyn Shaw, considered to be running props, had been in Welsh teams just before me without managing to pick up such a score. For this game the Pontypool front row was chosen *en bloc* to tighten the scrummage (Bobby Windsor and Charlie Faulkner being the other two) and the try came my way.

On the Welsh 25 Geoff Wheel hacked the ball away in the direction of a group of Frenchmen. None of them fell on the ball to kill it (they are not particularly keen on that sort of thing) and I kept going forward and soon found myself inside the French half with the ball still loose but the opposition full-back Taffary closing in. Under pressure from J. J. Williams, however, he completely misjudged his attempt to clear and the ball seemed to deflect from my team-mate's boot into my hands. I took it over with not a defender in sight.

The poker-faced reaction of our coach John Dawes was to ask why I hadn't gone round behind the posts!

MOST MEMORABLE TRY WITNESSED
Wales (32) v Ireland (4), Cardiff, 15.3.1975

If only for the expression on his face, I'd choose Charlie Faulkner's try in this game. It gave me terrific pleasure to see him crashing over after Bobby Windsor had popped the ball up to him — a case of a prop appreciating another prop.

Now all four of us forwards from the same club (Terry Cobner and Bobby himself being the others) had scored for Wales. Charlie was a great mate. And that ear-to-ear grin . . .

(Opposite)
Graham Price scored an unlikely try for a prop, running some 70 yards to do so in the 1975 France v. Wales match.

John Pullin
(Bristol, England & British Isles)
42 caps for England (1966-76), 7 Tests for the
British Isles (1968-71) as a hooker.
Now lives at Aust, near Bristol.

MOST MEMORABLE TRY SCORED
**England (11) v South Africa (8), Twickenham,
20.12.1969**

We were trailing the Springboks by eight points
to six with only 12 minutes of the match left. A
line-out took place on the opposition's line,
where their forwards took the ball and a ruck
formed. When the ball finally emerged on the
South African side I was able to touch it down
for my one and only try for England, with
Springbok skipper Dawie de Villiers protesting
loudly to the referee that I was offside. Impossible!

We then held on for England's first-ever
victory over South Africa.

MOST MEMORABLE TRY WITNESSED
**Canterbury (3) v British Isles (14), Christchurch,
19.6.1971**

This was a game in which the forwards spent
most of the afternoon involved in a punch-up
and looking over our shoulders to see where the
next fist was coming from.

Just before half-time the Lions managed to
put John Bevan in possession. As our wing got
the ball there were about half a dozen Canterbury players between him and the line. Despite
his great speed, he had no chance of outflanking them, so putting his head down he knocked
the first two or three would-be tacklers out of
the way and ploughed over Canterbury's line
with three more defenders draped round his
neck.

Derek Quinnell
(Llanelli, Wales & British Isles)
23 caps for Wales (1972-80), 5 Tests for British
Isles (1971-80) as a lock and back-row forward.
Now lives in Llanelli.

MOST MEMORABLE PARTICIPATION IN TRIES
Llanelli (9) v South Africa (10), Llanelli, 20.1.1970

The try scored by Llanelli midway through the
second half was great by any standards. It began
near our line and was rounded off at the other
end by Alun Richards after most of our team
had handled.

It lives on in my memory for many reasons,
not least that the Springboks were near to Test
strength that day, whereas Llanelli were actually short of two key men, Phil Bennett and
Delme Thomas, who had withdrawn because
they were due to play for Wales the following
Saturday. As a matter of fact we fielded no
capped players, though there was a lot of
potential in the team, which started a good
period in the Scarlets' history. Also, the match
was my first against a major touring side of such
calibre.

New Zealand (3) v British Isles (13), Wellington, 31.7.1971

From a line-out on the New Zealand 25 Gareth
Edwards burst away and kept Bob Burgess at
bay with a devastating hand-off before slipping
Barry John a scoring pass almost beneath the
All Blacks' crossbar. The conversion put the
Lions 13-0 up and proved that if we could score
tries like that we were good enough to win the
series.

This was my first-ever Test match. I had not
even been capped by Wales at this stage in my
career and had never met an All Black team —
so here was the real McCoy! Even to be selected
to play in the game gave me a great deal of
personal confidence.

Chris Rea

(West of Scotland, Headingley, Scotland & British Isles)
13 caps for Scotland (1968-71) as a centre.
Now lives in Edinburgh.

MOST MEMORABLE TRY SCORED
England (15) v Scotland (16), Twickenham, 20.3.1971

Scotland, 15-11 down with injury time approaching, won a ruck outside England's 25, scrum-half Duncan Peterson broke and passed to the Scottish captain Peter Brown. He sent an overhead pass to me which I collected and ran in for a try which he himself converted in his own inimitable style.

The five points gave Scotland a first victory at Twickenham since 1938.

Chris Rea showing the determination which helped him to score a crucial try in the 1971 Calcutta Cup match.

A. M. (Arthur) Rees

(London Welsh & Wales)
13 caps for Wales (1934-38) as a back-row forward.
Now lives at Ellenhall, Staffordshire.

MOST MEMORABLE PARTICIPATION IN TRY
Wales (13) v New Zealand (12), Cardiff, 21.12.1935

I was leading the Welsh forwards in a hectic battle for supremacy which was slowly going our way. Early in the second half, however, we had lost our hooker Donald Tarr with a broken neck.

At a line-out on half-way I made a two-handed catch and delivered clean, quick possession to Haydn Tanner who gave Cliff Jones a flying start with a lovely long ball. The 'mighty atom' made a half break and fed Wilfred Wooler who galloped through the defence at top speed and kicked over the full-back's head. I was just to Wilfred's left, but the ball bounced over him and away from me. But calmly following up was Geoffrey Rees-Jones who scored an unconverted try at the corner. With seven forwards playing like demons and Vivian Jenkins and Idwal Rees taking high balls safely under pressure we held on for victory.

I choose this try for its importance to Welsh Rugby. In 1905 Wales had won through a very, very controversial try still disputed by our friends in New Zealand. In 1924 the All Blacks won, and the whole of my youth was spent in the awareness of Wales 1, New Zealand 1. So the 1935 match was regarded as a 'decider'.

MOST MEMORABLE TRY WITNESSED
Wales (13) v New Zealand (8), Cardiff, 19.12.1953

For some reason I was sitting on a bench beside the touch-line at this match, not in the old internationals' sector in the stand, and although things were not going well for Wales I was enjoying the play of one of my protégés, wing forward Clem Thomas (his father and mine were great friends and said of their sons 'Their brains are mostly in their feet') who was in great form. Suddenly he received a pass right in front of us and was hemmed in. 'Get out of that, Clement,' I remarked to my companions. I could see his facial expression — he was thinking the same thing! He cross-kicked, more with hope than purpose, perhaps, but it was a beauty. That winger of more caps than passes, Ken Jones, swooped on it as he flew towards the line for a great try made out of a now almost forsaken tactic. Not a great one, maybe — not a wing beating man after man, but a favourite one of mine, made and scored by two great friends.

Hika Reid

(Bay of Plenty & New Zealand)
5 Tests for New Zealand (1980-83) as a hooker.
Now lives at Rotorua, New Zealand.

MOST MEMORABLE TRY SCORED
Australia (9) v New Zealand (12), Brisbane, 28.6.1980

At a maul which developed some ten metres from New Zealand's line I ripped the ball clear and set off upfield before serving our scrum-half Dave Loveridge. He passed to Bruce Robertson who made more ground before finding Gary Cunningham in close support. Tim Twigden, Andy Haden, Murray Watts and Murray Taylor all handled the ball before I received it again to run in and round the movement off.

I choose this try because, quite simply, it was one of the really great ones in New Zealand's Rugby history. Also it was my first try in an All Black jersey, and by sealing victory for the All Blacks it kept the Test series alive at 1-1.

MOST MEMORABLE TRY WITNESSED
Barbarians (23) v New Zealand (11) 1973

Sorry, but the one by Gareth Edwards in this game cannot be matched. It was a marvellous team try, but with individual brilliance also displayed by the players participating. Furthermore I remember it particularly well because it was scored against the All Blacks.

David Richards

(Swansea, Wales & British Isles)
17 caps for Wales (1979-83), 1 Test for British Isles (1980) as a centre.
Now lives at Porthcawl, Mid Glamorgan.

MOST MEMORABLE PARTICIPATION IN TRY
South African Invitation XV (19) v British Isles (22), Potchefstroom, 21.5.1980

I choose Mike Slemen's try because, coming after 72 minutes of play at a stage when the Lions were behind 16-19, it enabled us to keep our unbeaten tour record intact.

On a personal note I was particularly pleased at being able to initiate the movement and moreover was involved in it — that is, I handled the ball — on six separate occasions. However, it was also an outstanding team effort.

MOST MEMORABLE TRY WITNESSED
Wales (35) v Scotland (12), Cardiff, 5.2.1972

I choose Gareth Edwards's try for its outstanding individuality. So many things could have gone wrong, especially concerning the behaviour of the ball, but they didn't. Marvellous try!

Andy Ripley

(Rosslyn Park, England & British Isles)
24 caps for England (1972-76) as a number eight.
Now lives in London.

MOST MEMORABLE TRY SCORED
**England (16) v Wales (12), Twickenham,
16.3.1974**

My second-half score came from a five-yard
scrum not far from the Welsh posts where I
picked up and ran very close to the scrum for a
try which Alan Old easily converted. England
had taken the lead and lost it, but after this we
held on for a first win over Wales in 11 years. To
score was very satisfying, particularly against a
back row comprising Mervyn Davies, Terry
Cobner and Dai Morris.

MOST MEMORABLE TRY WITNESSED
**Moseley (19) v Invitation XV (43), Moseley,
27.11.1977**

The Sam Doble Memorial match turned out to
be a great game played in a terrific atmosphere
at the Reddings, albeit a sad occasion in memory
of a great guy who had given a lot to the game.
Though not playing I was very happy to be in
attendance on an autumn afternoon when the
Rugby was of a high quality. Gerald Davies's
final try, for which he sped through the defence
with a series of each-way side-steps, rounded
things off in fine style.

Beverley Risman

(Loughborough Colleges, England, & British Isles)
8 caps for England (1959-61), 4 Tests for British
Isles (1959).
Now lives at Crowthorne, Berkshire.

MOST MEMORABLE TRY SCORED
**New Zealand (6) v British Isles (9), Auckland,
19.9.1959**

With 16 minutes left of the Lions' farewell
match Down Under, the score stood at 6-6. We
won a scrummage near the left touch-line and
some 40 yards from the All Blacks' posts.
Inside-half Andy Mulligan ran to the open side,
drawing the opposing back row with him,
before switching the ball to me. Finding the way
forward blocked I ran back down the blind side
of the breaking scrum and side-stepped the lone
defender, wing Bruce McPhail.

At this point, amazingly, my path to the line
lay completely open, with the cover defence out
of position. Speed was the essential thing — and
I had enough to outflank would-be tacklers and
avoid full-back Don Clarke's despairing dive to
score in the left-hand corner. The conversion
attempt failed but the Lions won by three tries
to two penalty goals.

The British Isles considered themselves un-
lucky to lose the First Test (17-18, with six
penalties kicked for New Zealand by Clarke)
and the Second (8-11). My decisive and winning
try seemed to vindicate our view that we could
have won the series.

MOST MEMORABLE TRY WITNESSED
**England (15) v Ireland (16), Twickenham,
6.2.1982**

The Irish began an attack from some 35 metres'
range with quick passing towards the right
touch-line. Despite close attention from several
defenders the ball was kept alive and worked
back inside to Ollie Campbell, who had initiated
the movement. The stand-off did outstandingly
well under pressure to slip possession to prop
'Ginger' McLoughlin, now within the England
22. He was checked by two or three attempted
tackles, whereupon almost the whole pack
formed a driving wedge to sweep him over in
the corner.

This try exhibited many of the best things in the game — quick passing, good support play, a dash of genius and finally a superb forward drive with all the fire and aggression of a great Irish pack combining as an unstoppable unit.

Peter Robbins
(Moseley & England)
19 caps for England (1956-62) as a flanker.
Now lives in West Midlands.

MOST MEMORABLE PARTICIPATION IN TRY
England (9) v Australia (6), Twickenham, 1.2.1958

In scoring the injury-time try which won the game Peter Jackson did not display any great pace but, when hemmed in, showed terrific skill to elude defenders and pull the game out of the fire for England against the odds.

I choose his try because this was a Test we desperately wanted to win. Also, since we were down to 14 men I was an emergency centre and had a hand in the move which sent the ball along the line and led to our try.

MOST MEMORABLE TRY WITNESSED
Wales (35) v Scotland (12), Cardiff, 5.2.1972

In Gareth Edwards's second try, scored at the right-hand corner after a great run down the south touch-line, there was encapsulated all that Rugby football should be: strength, speed, determination, courage, bravado, skill — even wit. From the onlookers' point of view Edwards created something wholly unexpected which led to high drama.

Such was the try's devastating effect that after it the match was as good as settled.

Ian Robertson

(London Scottish, Watsonians & Scotland)
8 caps for Scotland (1968-70) as a stand-off half.
Now lives in London.

Peter Dods – scorer of the most inspired of the five tries which sank Ireland and gave Scotland the Triple Crown in 1984.

MOST MEMORABLE TRY SCORED
Wales (18) v Scotland (9), Cardiff, 7.2.1970

Until the early eighties Scotland had not enjoyed the best of results against Wales at Cardiff and in the first half of this 1970 match it looked as if we might upset the odds with a vengeance. Playing with the wind I had dropped a goal to gain the lead for Scotland. Then after 25 minutes J. P. R. Williams failed to find touch with a clearance and I gathered the ball near the half-way line, heading off down the north stand touch-line towards the city end of the ground. After some snappy interpassing I was up to take a final pass, sell a dummy and score in the corner.

The special atmosphere of an international match at Cardiff tends to live longer than that of any other stadium in the world and it had always been my dream to score a try there. So this was the happiest single moment of my career — and I'm still waiting hopefully for Max Boyce to record the event in song.

MOST MEMORABLE TRY WITNESSED
Ireland (9) v Scotland (32), Dublin, 3.3.1984

I choose the try by Peter Dods at the end of the match. It gave Scotland their first Triple Crown since 1938 and put them three-quarters of the way to a second Grand Slam, and this historical significance is part of the reason for my choice. As with a small boy who gets only one ice-cream each summer, the taste of success is heightened when it is isolated and unexpected.

Secondly, I have long abhorred the regimentation and discipline of Rugby in the eighties. It has become part of the computer age, with players little more than automatons enacting programmes devised by coaches. So it was a pleasure to see four of the five Scottish tries on this day in Dublin scored directly from set-piece possession. The Dods try was the most inspired of these, giving encouragement to those who believe in the creative skills of individuals rather than the much less inspired method and percentage Rugby which has overtaken the modern game.

Clive Rowlands

(Pontypool & Wales)
14 caps for Wales (1963-65) as a scrum-half.
Now lives at Upper Cwmtwrch, West Glamorgan.

MOST MEMORABLE PARTICIPATION IN TRY
Wales (14) v England (3), Cardiff, 16.1.1963

This game was on the old wet and muddy Cardiff Arms Park, never an easy surface on which to play well in the middle of winter. We led 3-0 at half-time and were anxious to build up our lead without delay as the second half opened.

Our pack did well at a series of rucks and mauls 40 yards out, allowing a rush to develop down the right spearheaded by Norman Gale. Denzil Williams took up the running and gave on to Brian Price, who just failed to reach the line. The other forwards all piled in, generating tremendous momentum, before Brian Thomas in typical fashion ripped possession clear. I gave to David Watkins, and the ball travelled briskly via John Uzzell and John Dawes to Stuart Watkins who ran it in.

It was a classic try in difficult conditions, with each man doing his job correctly. As it turned out it set us on course not just for victory over England but also towards a Triple Crown.

MOST MEMORABLE TRY WITNESSED
France (5) v Wales (9), Paris, 27.3.1971

Barry John got the try, gliding through the French defence from a set scrum 15 yards from the French posts, but as he himself said afterwards it was made possible by Wales's hooker Jeff Young who took a strike against the head. It was the first he'd struck for in the entire game — and he won it.

As the Welsh team's coach I approved of its simplicity, which stemmed from the effort put into a crucial scrum. Thus the try can be attributed not just to a player's individual skill but also to the work of all eight forwards.

Stuart Watkins – scorer of a classic try against England in 1963.

Don Rutherford

(Gloucester, England & British Isles)
14 caps for England (1960-67), 1 Test for British
Isles (1966) as a full-back.
Now Technical Officer to RFU at Twickenham.

MOST MEMORABLE TRY WITNESSED
France (15) v England (27), Paris, 20.2.1982

The game was some fifteen minutes old, and it
seemed inevitable that France must score following a grub-kick across the England goal-line
where, after a desperate race, John Carleton
just beat the attackers to the touchdown. The
pressure was off and with the exception of just
four players — three Englishmen and a Frenchman — all present imagined that a 22-metre
drop-out was about to take place. Members of
the French team actually turned their backs on
the play.

Suddenly Carleton threw the ball to Paul
Dodge who was standing just inside the field of
play. He tossed the ball forward to Mike Slemen
on the 22-metre line. My initial reaction was,
'What on earth is he doing, trying a quick
drop-out in this situation — he's bound to make
a mistake!' O ye of little faith!

Slemen's drop kick was of the grubber variety,
travelling towards the England 10-metre line.
Just as it looked certain to be intercepted by a
covering Frenchman Clive Woodward appeared
on Slemen's inside shoulder, and between them
they propelled the ball another 20 metres or so
forward away from France's left-wing Laurent
Pardoe who was in hot pursuit. Woodward had
the honour of giving the ball its final propulsion
before diving onto it between the goalposts.

This try looked straightforward in its execu-
tion. Yet it required vision, initiative, speed, and
considerable ball control. It demonstrated con-
clusively that counter-attack is a most potent
weapon.

John Rutherford

(Selkirk, Scotland & British Isles)
28 caps for Scotland (1979-84) as a stand-off half,
1 Test for British Isles (1983) as a centre.
Now lives in Edinburgh.

MOST MEMORABLE PARTICIPATION IN TRY
Wales (18) v Scotland (34), Cardiff, 20.3.1984

I specifically enjoyed and remember Scotland's
first try not only because it was spectacular but
because it swung the game our way. Wales
seemed to be all over us for the first 20 minutes
but had only a penalty goal to show for their
pressure. Then a loose ball reached Gareth
Davies who, instead of moving it to the wing,
kicked ahead. It was not a bad kick but the ball
bounced kindly for Scotland and Roger Baird
began the move which ended with Jim Calder
touching down.

This try not only gave Scotland the lead but
instilled into us the confidence necessary for any
side to win at Cardiff Arms Park.

MOST MEMORABLE TRY WITNESSED
England (23) v Scotland (17), Twickenham, 21.2.1981

I remember this try because it came from
nothing and showed the tremendous individual
skills of Clive Woodward. Scotland seemed to
have him well covered but amazingly Clive beat
several forwards and eventually cut inside
Bruce Hay to score the best individual try I have
ever seen.

R. W. H. (Bob) Scott

(Auckland & New Zealand)

17 Tests for New Zealand (1946-54) as a full-back.
Now lives in North Tairua, New Zealand.

MOST MEMORABLE PARTICIPATION IN TRY
New Zealand (6) v British Isles (3), Wellington, 1.7.1950

The climax to this game was full of drama because of several injuries, in particular that suffered by the All Black captain and second five-eighth Ron Elvidge. He was taken off late in the first half with a badly gashed eye and a severe chest injury (and did not play again for New Zealand).

When, obviously still in pain, he returned to the field after half-time to play a roving game, the All Blacks were behind 3-0 and down to six forwards. Our prop Simpson had left the field with an injured knee (never to play again) and loose forward Peter Johnstone was standing in for the injured Elvidge in the back-line and continued to do so after the latter's return.

Still New Zealand managed to mount an attack. I joined the back-line to make an extra man and passed to Roy Roper. Knowing how badly injured Elvidge was, our centre missed him out and gave to the forward Johnstone. But the captain, determined to be in the movement, switched outside Johnstone who was then obliged to pass him the ball. Elvidge covered the remaining ten yards to the line and crashed over Billy Cleaver, the Lions' very determined last line of defence, for a try which I consider the most courageous I have ever witnessed.

I choose the try for the bravery and determination of the scorer — and because I have always felt pride that I was in the movement.

MOST MEMORABLE TRY WITNESSED.
New Zealand (11) v British Isles (8), Auckland, 29.7.1950

This try, by Ken Jones, was superb: perfectly executed, unexpected, against the run of play — and scored by a wing who still remains in my memory as one of the great players. I witnessed the try coming and going, you might say.

The setting was perfect: a clear blue sky, no wind, a final Test match between the All Blacks and a Lions XV still recognized as the most brilliant side to visit New Zealand. With ten minutes left the British Isles were 11—3 down, and New Zealand on the attack. Lewis Jones, the Lions' full-back, received a pass almost on his own line and broke the All Black line. Confronted by me he gave to Ken Jones who stepped inside our left-wing Peter Henderson and set off for the line some 75 yards away pursued by all 15 of the New Zealand team. They could not catch him.

The daring of Lewis Jones sparked the opportunity, but then it was the football brain and balance of Ken Jones as he moved inside Henderson which made the try. It must have been one of the most spectacular tries ever seen by the 60,000 privileged to be at Eden Park that day. Oh to have seen it on TV — and the replay!

Richard Sharp

(Oxford University, Redruth, Wasps, England and British Isles)
14 caps for England (1960-67), 2 Tests for British Isles (1962) at stand-off half.
Now lives at St. Austell, Cornwall.

MOST MEMORABLE TRY SCORED
England (16) v Ireland (0), Twickenham, 10.2.1962

The try for which I am usually remembered was the one I scored against Scotland at Twickenham in 1963. This has been shown on TV so many times that people have forgotten that I did score on other occasions!

The try which gave me the most satisfaction and the performance which yielded most pleasure came in England's game against Ireland in 1962. Before the match Stan Hodgson, our superb hooker from Durham, had said to me that he would do his best 'to win a few against the head', adding: 'You must do the rest, Richard, and score a try from one of them.'

With minutes remaining England were leading 11-0 when, true to his word, Stan won yet another strike against the head. The Irish defence was taken by surprise and I was able to get past the tacklers and run round behind the posts for a try which I converted myself.

It was Stan's great skill which had made the score possible. Hookers rarely got themselves on the score sheet in those days, but a heel against the head was something very special. On that day, much to Stan's and my delight, it had worked well.

Richard Sharp remembers most fondly his try in the 1962 England v. Ireland match, following a strike against the head by Stan Hodgson.

Kevin Skinner

(Otago, Counties & New Zealand)
20 Tests for New Zealand (1949-56) as a prop.
Now lives in Auckland, New Zealand.

Mike Slemen

(Liverpool, England & British Isles)
29 caps for England (1976-82), 1 Test for British
Isles (1980) as a wing.
Now lives in Crosby, Lancashire.

MOST MEMORABLE TRY SCORED
**Australia (11) v New Zealand (17), Sydney,
23.6.1951**

The New Zealand full-back Cockerill kicked for
touch to the Australian corner where his opposite number Tooth could only get a hand to the
ball as it went out of play, thus giving us the
throw-in. Jarden and I were first on the spot, he
threw to me, and I had a stroll of a couple of
yards for a try awarded by Aussie referee H. A.
Tolhurst.

Then all hell broke loose. The ball that was
kicked out was still among the mob on the Hill.
Jarden had thrown me the spare ball which he
grabbed off the ball boy — but in those days
decisions were made and adhered to, so the try
stood. I may add that every time I subsequently
appeared at Sydney, especially in front of the
Hill, I was roasted.

I choose this try because it was the only one I
scored in a Test match!

MOST MEMORABLE PARTICIPATION IN TRY
**New Zealand (11) v South Africa (5), Auckland,
1.9.1956**

After Ron Hemi had burst through the front of
the line-out and kicked infield, flanker Peter
Jones picked up the loose ball. Then about 17
stones in weight, which in those days was extra
big, he quickly got into full flight and broke
clear to run in from about 25 yards' range. I
rather suspect that the odd Springbok back was
not too interested in making the tackle.

I choose this try because it sealed the match
and the Test series for New Zealand. It was my
last Test and, after four defeats in South Africa
on the 1949 visit, we had now been involved in a
great series which put the All Blacks back on top
of the ladder.

MOST MEMORABLE TRY SCORED
**South African Invitation XV (19) v British Isles
(22), Potchefstroom, 21.5.1980**

At altitude, in heat and against a 'loaded'
midweek side the British Isles came back from
the brink of defeat to save the match in style. In
a game that had been dominated by kicking we
began to run the ball on our 22. The movement
continued for one minute, 36 seconds without a
break, the ball being handled by 33 players. I
was the last, and ran in the try.

After I scored it did not immediately occur to
me that the move had gone on for so long. It
was only after the final whistle that the players
began to realize that we had been part of
something special. What sticks in my mind is the
ball-winning ability of Derek Quinnell and the
South Africans' covering and tackling.

MOST MEMORABLE TRY WITNESSED
**England (23) v Scotland (17), Twickenham,
21.2.1981**

From a line-out Clive Woodward came back on
a scissors move with his stand-off half. In the
space of 20 metres he beat at least four men on
his run to score.

I pick this try as it was a piece of individual
brilliance from a set-piece, where as often as not
the ball would have been set up for the
forwards.

D. W. C. (Doug) Smith

(London Scottish, Scotland & British Isles)
8 caps for Scotland (1949-53), 1 Test for British
Isles (1950) as a wing. Manager, British Isles,
1971.
Now lives in Orsett, Essex.

MOST MEMORABLE TRY SCORED
Scotland (6) v Wales (5), Murrayfield, 5.2.1949

Intercepting near the half-way line, I dashed off
chased by my opposite number Ken Jones with
Hamish Dawson, a front-row forward on my
inside and the touch-line a foot away on the
other side. I suppose it really could have been a
case of obstruction, but no matter — I scored in
the mists of Murrayfield and Scotland won!

MOST MEMORABLE TRIES WITNESSED
Hawkes Bay (6) v British Isles (25), Napier,
17.7.1971

In this game I saw four of the most wonderful
tries, scored by a great wing — Gerald Davies.

To describe them I would require the descrip-
tive powers and words of Dylan Thomas and
Carwyn James, the greatest coach in the world.
So let me just say that these were four tries that
will live in my memory for ever.

A. G. (Tony) Steel

(Canterbury & New Zealand)
9 Tests for New Zealand
(1966-68) as a wing.
Now lives in Hamilton, New Zealand.

MOST MEMORABLE TRIES SCORED
East Wales (3) v New Zealand (3), Cardiff,
13.12.1967

My equalizing try was memorable because with
only 11 minutes left we were trailing 3-0. I have
never played for an All Black side whose
forwards were so outgunned and which had to
do so much defending and covering throughout
the whole course of a match. Conditions were
still atrocious after snow which had caused a
four-day postponement from the previous
Saturday.

One reason I have for choosing this try is the
difference between the way it really happened
and the way it was described in the Press —
'sheer brilliance', 'great individuality', 'Masterly
sense of balance' were among the expressions
used. What follows is the way I remember it.

Late in the game our forwards finally won a
ruck. Chris Laidlaw not being in attendance,
someone — it may have been Brian Lochore —
sent a pass to our left where we were thin on the
ground, Gerald Kember and myself being
marked by a full set of East Wales backs.
Kember received and set himself to heave the
ball, which was very heavy by this stage, to me.
Seeing that it would not carry, I moved infield at
the last moment to catch it. This sudden change
of direction, simply to obtain possession, left two
East Wales backs in the mud and was described
by the Press as the 'brilliant beating of two men'!

I then headed for the green grass in the
five-yard area, using it to elude the defenders,
who were stuck in the mud, and reach the line.
What was described as 'brilliant' was thus simply
a matter of survival.

Barbarians (6) v New Zealand (11), Twickenham,
16.12.1967

Three days after the East Wales game I scored
at the close of our final tour game in Britain at
Twickenham. The try itself was fairly straightforward: simply a kick by Stewart Wilson, the

Barbarians' full-back, which failed to go out and was collected by Brian Lochore. He drew a man and, going slightly infield, passed to Earl Kirton who followed suit and set me up for the final run-in. In many ways the try was a soft one; it was the build-up and the circumstances which make it memorable.

The All Blacks were handling badly, we were behind at 6-3 and the many lost opportunities were jeopardizing our chances of an unbeaten record. But, probably as a result, the tempo of the game increased over the last 20 minutes, getting faster and faster, harder and harder, until it seemed to me that something just had to give.

With three minutes left I could see that we were about to win a ruck and decided to move into the back-line to try and make a break to rescue the game. I got the ball, broke the defence, and came onto Wilson at full-back. Looking to my right I saw Ian MacRae and was in two minds: should I hang onto the ball because of some indifferent handling by him hitherto or should I obey the prompting of all my Rugby training which told me to draw a defender and pass to the man outside?

As a result I did the really inexcusable, selling a half-hearted dummy and allowing Wilson to tip me off balance. Knowing that I was on the verge of blowing it I desperately sent a soft, lobbed pass in the direction of Ian who caught it and scored. What was to be the beginning of my favourite few moments in an All Black jersey could have ended with disaster — but hadn't!

As I ran back to half-way I knew how close I had been to making the biggest goof of my life. When the conversion attempt failed I was bitterly disappointed that the result was set to be a draw and desperately hoped that play would be restarted.

I have a feeling that the referee was enjoying the occasion and wanted one more minute. He allowed the Barbarians to kick off and, though desperately anxious to run the ball in a final attempt to score winning points, the All Blacks erred and had to scrummage against a Baa-Baas' put-in. Hooker Angus McLeod took a tight-head, Chris Laidlaw put it high in the air for Stewart Wilson to collect and feint to kick to his left for touch, our right. He then turned to kick the other way. The ball failed to go out, BJ did his bit, 'Conch' Kirton did his.

And the rest you know.

M. R. (Mickey) Steele-Bodger
(Cambridge University & England).
9 caps for England (1947-48) as a flanker.
Now lives in Tamworth, Staffordshire.

MOST MEMORABLE PARTICIPATION IN TRY
Barbarians (9) v Australia (6), Cardiff, 31.1.1948

This was a magnificent try from a set-piece. Following a scrum near the half-way line the Barbarians' scrum-half Haydn Tanner passed to Tommy Kemp who gave the ball almost immediately to Bleddyn Williams. Having made a half break he gave to his fellow centre Billy Cleaver, whose straightening of the line enabled Williams to loop around, take a return pass and send possession on to Martin Turner. Our wing was tackled just short of the line but at that moment Haydn Tanner, who had started the movement, appeared outside him, took his pass and scored the try — I believe that at the outset Haydn gave a dive pass, making it all the more remarkable that he could have got outside the wing to take a scoring pass!

I choose this try for several reasons. First, the game was billed as the 'match of the century', as the first-ever game between the Barbarians and a major touring side. The Wallabies had had a wonderful tour and had not had their line crossed in any international game — we scored three tries against them. Moreover those who saw both the 1948 match and the more famous one (because of greater media coverage) in 1973 when New Zealand were the Barbarians' opponents think that there was little to choose between the two.

MOST MEMORABLE TRY WITNESSED
Midland Counties (13) v RFU President's XV (18), Leicester, 8.4.1971

The Invitation XV, engaged in the first of four tour games to honour the Centenary of the RFU, was drawn from five nations and, after taking a lot of time to settle down, was behind with not much time left. Then, from a kick-off the giant South African lock Frik du Preez caught the ball and ran through more or less the whole opposition before scoring a try that won the match with at least two would-be tacklers clinging to him.

This was a magnificent effort from a forward who had already played hard for nearly 80 minutes. Most great tries seem to have been scored by backs who have more open space in which to display their art, but this try for me was made really memorable by the pace, power and aggression of a great lock. Brian Lochore, the All Black who had skippered the Invitation XV, gave Frik the presentation jersey he had just received as a gesture of respect and admiration.

Haydn Tanner
(Swansea, Cardiff, Wales & British Isles)
25 caps for Wales (1935-49), 1 Test for British Isles (1938) as a scrum-half.
Now lives at Thames Ditton, Surrey.

MOST MEMORABLE PARTICIPATION IN TRY
Wales (13) v New Zealand (12), Cardiff, 21.12.1935

By no stretch of the imagination could Geoffrey Rees-Jones's winning try be described as a classic illustrating the finer points of Rugby football. So, having been involved in many other tries of much greater technical merit, why do I prize the memory of this one above all?

(a) Wales versus New Zealand has a certain 'something' which no other international game possesses.

(b) The odds were stacked against us, with time running out and only 14 men on the field, Donald Tarr having been carried off. That was when Wilfred Wooler hoisted his kick-ahead and the cruel bounce beat all players but one. In parts the ground was frost-bound and it could well be that Rees-Jones, sensing that it could be a difficult bounce, held back to collect the ball and score.

(c) This was my first game for Wales and I was still at school. Victory in one's first international is sweet, but against New Zealand . . . What more could one ask?

(d) For me, the try clinched a 'double'. Three months earlier Swansea, with myself at scrum-half, had become the first-ever club side to defeat a New Zealand XV.

James W. (Jim) Telfer

(Melrose, Scotland & British Isles)
25 caps for Scotland (1964-70), 8 Tests for British
Isles (1966-68) as a number eight. Assistant
Manager, British Isles, 1973.
Now lives in Selkirk, Borders.

MOST MEMORABLE TRY SCORED
France (3) v Scotland (6), Paris, 11.1.1969

At a scrum on the French 10-yard line opposition scrum-half Berot was dispossessed by Ian
McCrae, who had come on for Gordon Connell
as the first-ever replacement in the Five Nations
Championship. He gave to Tom Elliott who in
turn passed to me. I then beat France's full-back
Pierre Villepreux to score.

The significance of this try is that from that
day until the time of writing Scotland have not
beaten France in Paris.

MOST MEMORABLE TRY WITNESSED
Wales (18) v Scotland (34), Cardiff, 20.3.1982

Wales were attacking, Gareth Davies kicking
into Scotland's 22 on the visitors' left. Roger
Baird took the ball on the touch-line and
counter-attacked, reaching the half-way line
before passing to Iain Paxton. Tackled on the
Welsh 22, Paxton passed to Alan Tomes, who
gave a scoring pass near the line to Jim Calder.

I choose this try because the move started in
Scotland's 22 where Roger Baird showed a very
positive attitude to attack. The support and
running from then on was first class.

*Jim Calder finished off a brilliant counter-attack by the Scots at
Cardiff Arms Park in 1982.*

Malcolm Thomas

(Devonport Services, Newport, Wales & British Isles)
27 caps for Wales (1949-59), 4 Tests for British Isles (1950-59) as a centre and wing.
Now lives in Beaconsfield, Buckinghamshire.

MOST MEMORABLE TRY SCORED
Ireland (3) v Wales (6), Belfast, 11.3.1950

Wales were seeking the Triple Crown in Ireland. We had beaten England at Twickenham and Scotland at Swansea, where partnering Jack Matthews at centre, I had scored a try in the corner.

In the evening after that game the chairman of selectors took me aside to ask if I would play against Ireland on the left wing. So it was that I found myself alongside my Devonport Services colleague Lewis Jones at Ravenhill Park with four minutes left of a match poised to end as a three-all draw.

The Irish won a scrum inside their own half and as stand-off half Jackie Kyle got the ball he was caught by Billy Cleaver and Ray Cale. The ball ran loose for Cleaver to play it with his foot and send out a swift pass to Lewis Jones. Beautifully balanced and sure of hand, he moved almost lazily into full stride. With a faint body swerve he invited Lane, the Irish wing, towards him. Then, at exactly the right moment, he threw a high overhead pass which I took above my head and charged for the corner.

All the long years of Welsh schoolboy coaching were packed into that final thrust for the corner. As I grounded the ball I knew it was a try but Ireland's full-back George Norton, in his attempt at a tackle, missed me and took the corner flag. The touch judge was an Irishman and an international referee, Ossie Glasgow, and our supporters held their breath. But not for long. Running behind the posts he marked an historic point in Welsh Rugby fortunes: victory for Wales and a first Triple Crown since 1911!

R. C. C. (Clem) Thomas

(Cambridge University, Swansea, Wales & British Lions)
26 caps for Wales (1949-59), 2 Tests for the British Isles (1955) as a flanker.
Now lives in Gower, West Glamorgan.

MOST MEMORABLE PARTICIPATION IN TRY
Wales (13) v New Zealand (8), Cardiff, 19.12.1953

Having appeared to be a beaten team for most of the second half we were brought level through a successful penalty when the All Black 'Snow' White was caught offside. At 8-8 Wales had the ghost of a chance with 15 minutes left.

Now, crucially, an opponent failed to take a high ball on the Welsh left. Some loose exchanges ensued, resulting in my picking up and making some 15 yards' headway within the New Zealand half where the alert cover defence cornered me. Twice I went to release the ball to support players, twice there was nothing on, twice I retained possession while two or three All Blacks bought dummies.

Then I noticed that the midfield was wide open and glimpsed Ken Jones, our right-wing, in the distance. I kicked in his direction. The high bounce beat Ron Jarden. Ken swept past, steadied himself to take the ball, accelerated and cut inside to score at the posts. The conversion went over and Cardiff Arms Park went crazy — there must have been hundreds of lost hats!

Although I realized the value of the try, I did not appreciate quite how good it was, or what people thought about it, until I read the newspapers next day. The risk, incidentally, was very great, for had Ken not been speedy enough to intercept my cross-kick, Ron Jarden could have gathered and sprinted away unmarked to score against Wales!

MOST MEMORABLE TRY WITNESSED
South African Invitation XV (19) v British Isles (22), Potchefstroom, 21.5.1980

The try initiated by David Richards and finished off a minute and a half later by Mike Slemen was the greatest I have ever seen for accumulative excitement. It embodied most of what is best in Rugby football, and was also a winning try enabling the Lions to come from behind to clinch the match.

Peter Thompson

(Headingley, Waterloo & England)
17 caps for England (1956-59) as a wing.
Now lives at Haywards Heath, Sussex.

MOST MEMORABLE TRY *NOT* SCORED
Leicester (6) v Barbarians (23), Leicester,
26.12.1956

It was a very ordinary 'try'. I had only to dive over the line after a footrush, managing to get both hands firmly on the ball as I slid over it (Christmas had been white). Imagine my surprise when the likeable John Clements came flying past to land with a whoop on the ball — and be given a try by referee Dudley Kemp. My try! Anyway, you didn't argue with referees then. It wasn't done (and you still called them 'Sir').

Why do I choose this try? I had already scored five, so it would have given me a Barbarians' record which I now have to share with Tom Barber, C. B. Holmes and David Duckham. But with a back-line reading Terry Davies, myself, Gareth Griffiths, Gordon Wells, Tony O'Reilly, Cliff Morgan and Andy Mulligan who could fail to score tries?

MOST MEMORABLE PARTICIPATION IN TRY
England (9) v Australia (6), Twickenham, 1.2.1958

In the dying moments of the game the score was 6-6. I threw in on the left and the ball was swiftly moved to Peter Jackson who looked completely hemmed in. Casually, it seemed to me, he ran 25 yards to the line for a winning try. He wasn't fast; but nobody could get hold of him, even though they knew he was going to side-step.

John Thornett

(New South Wales & Australia)
37 Tests for Australia (1955-67) as prop.
Now lives in Mosman, Australia.

MOST MEMORABLE PARTICIPATION IN TRY
Barbarians (11) v Australia (17), Cardiff,
28.1.1967

This was the last game of the Wallabies' 1966-67 tour of the United Kingdom. On a fairly muddy track Australia led all the way until ten minutes from time when our full-back J. K. Lenehan held back Stuart Watkins who had kicked ahead over the goal-line. A penalty try was awarded to put us behind 9-11.

Immediately upon the restart we won the first maul and Lenehan joined the back-line for wing Webb to be stopped just short in the left-hand corner. Our pack got there quickly and won the ruck. Again Lenehan made the extra man to send Stuart Boyce over in the right-hand corner. The ovation was the loudest I ever experienced — so much so that I looked up at the crowd to see, I believe, every person standing and clapping.

Because of his size, speed, capacity for straight running, and judgment about when to play the role, Lenehan was a very effective extra in the back-line. His great effort on this occasion compensated for an earlier error, retrieved the game for us and brought the tour to a very happy conclusion in front of that splendid Cardiff crowd.

Mark Titley
(Bridgend & Wales)
5 caps for Wales (1983-1984) as a wing.
Now lives in Cardiff, South Glamorgan.

MOST MEMORABLE TRY SCORED
Bridgend (6) v Pontypool (16), Bridgend, 24.9.1983

It is tempting to choose my first try for Wales, scored against Scotland in January 1984. However, as it was set up by the pack and our scrum-half Mark Douglas it does not figure in my personal list of best achievements.

Instead I select a try I got against Pontypool in a club game — when we took a hammering from the Gwent side. In one of our rare entries into their half the ball came perfectly along the line giving me just enough space to run at my opposite number and lose him with an outside swerve. The visitors' highly experienced full-back Peter Lewis was now coming across on collision course, and I checked him with the suggestion of an inside jink before going for the outside gap. There was just enough space, and I went all the way to the line from about 40 metres out.

MOST MEMORABLE PARTICIPATION IN DISALLOWED TRY
Pontypool (18) v Bridgend (16), Pontypool 28.1.1984

In this Schweppes Cup tie on the home ground of the then holders of the trophy, Bridgend's best hope seemed to be running the ball and tangling as little as possible with their formidable pack. In keeping with this policy we brought the ball away from our 22 through a scissors move between myself and stand-off half David Thomas. Ritchie Griffiths, Howell Davies and myself kept up the momentum and supplied speedy Glen Webbe with a scoring pass just inside the Pontypool half. He outstripped the cover and reached the line with room to spare. The whole Bridgend XV, especially those of us up with the ball, were astonished when the referee brought us back to half-way and awarded Pontypool the put-in at a set scrum for a forward pass.

I've studied the video of the game umpteen times and still can't accept that decision. Had the try beem allowed we might have gone on to greater things. Instead we lost what turned into a battle of penalty goals.

Errol Tobias

(Boland, SARF & South Africa)
4 caps for South Africa (1983-84) as a stand-off half.
Now lives in Bergsig Caledon, South Africa.

MOST MEMORABLE PARTICIPATION IN TRIES
Cardiff (32) v Barbarians (32), Cardiff, 2.4.1983

As I went onto the field for this match I felt free. I had not been over-coached and had been told to play the way I wanted. 'Barbarians don't need coaches,' they said. 'It is just a case of 15 gifted players being thrown together to play Rugby football.' That brought out the best in me. I said to myself, 'I am going to take on my man no matter what.' Soon I opened up the play from the Barbarians' line, making about 45 metres in a curving run. Centre Danie Gerber was close at hand and took my pass to go in for a try from half-way.

Tries like that will keep Rugby alive. Certainly they are missing from Test matches, where midfield players do not believe in themselves. This is the fault of coaches, who are afraid to lose a match and order their backs to keep the ball in front of the forwards. Ten-man Rugby is the result.

New Zealand (25) v South Africa (22), Auckland, 12.9.1981

Players should learn to kick not to gain ground but to keep possession as Ray Mordt did with a try (his third of the match) which levelled the score at 19-19.

It was a one-to-one situation. Ray calmly chipped ahead. The bounce beat the full back, Ray gathered, and the try was there.

Danie Gerber in action for the Barbarians against Cardiff in 1983. After Tobias had made a decisive break, he ran in a try from half-way. 'Tries like that will keep Rugby alive.'

W. (Bunner) Travers

(Newport, Wales & British Lions)
12 caps for Wales (1937-49), 2 Tests for British Isles (1938) as a hooker.
Now lives in Newport, Gwent.

MOST MEMORABLE TRY SCORED
Wales (11) v Scotland (3), Cardiff, 4.2.1939

I came down the left touch-line from half-way leaving five or six Scots spreadeagled on the deck. The last of them put in his dive just as I crossed the line, his fingers running down my back. I knew then that I was clear and ran around to give Wilfred Wooller an easy kick at goal to ensure victory.

I had great joy from this because my father, who was disabled, was watching me play for Wales for the one and only time. He won 25 caps from Pill Harriers, a junior side in Newport.

MOST MEMORABLE PARTICIPATION IN TRY
Ireland (0) v Wales (7), Belfast, 11.3.1939

Having beaten England and Scotland, Ireland seemed set for a Triple Crown. Their forwards were very tall, persuading me as pack leader to opt for scrums frequently rather than lines-out — and my forwards scrummaged magnificently. At half-time we decided that we could carry on scrummaging hard and at the first scrum in the second half I shouted to Haydn Tanner to let Willie Davies have a drop at goal. He threw a beautiful pass and our stand-off half dropped the goal.

Encouraged by this, Willie ran through the whole Irish team a few minutes from the end for my favourite try. He thus scored all of our winning points.

Herbert Waddell

(Glasgow Academicals, Scotland & British Isles)
15 caps for Scotland (1924-30), 3 Tests for British Isles (1924) as a stand-off half.
Now lives in Glasgow.

MOST MEMORABLE PARTICIPATION IN TRIES
Scotland (14) v England (11), Murrayfield, 21.3.1925

The Scottish Rugby Union's new ground was being opened — but some way into the game England were in the lead. Then came a scrum a little way into our half on the east side of the pitch. Scotland won possession, my scrum-half Nelson sent me the ball and I passed to Macpherson, backing him up to take a return pass after he had cut through brilliantly and covered some 20 yards. When challenged by England's full-back Holliday, I gave to the supporting Nelson on my left with 25 yards to run.

But Holliday had turned and now threatened to overtake our scrum-half. Then it was that Nelson, a very strong man, managed to turn and hand him off between shoulder and neck before racing on to score at the posts. These first points from a Scot at Murrayfield could not have been scored by a better man.

The try is chosen because it was taken at tremendous pace with excellent backing up and good passing.

Ireland (8) v Scotland (14), Dublin, 28.2.1925

Our second try was started by a pass to myself from Nelson on the Scottish goal-line. I passed to Dykes, who sent Aitken off on a long run of 40 yards before transferring to Wallace. He was cut off near the Irish 25, where Aitken, Dykes and myself in turn bore the attack on. I finally gave a scoring pass to MacMyn who crossed between the posts. The Irish crowd cheered this try loudly, which was a remarkable event in an international match.

This try is chosen because it concluded a superb attack from our line, with fast, accurate passing and tremendous backing up.

Scotland (12) v Wales (9), Murraryfield, 1.2.1930

We were playing towards the river end when from a scrum on our right the ball reached our scrum-half Nelson. He passed to me and I passed to Macpherson. He cut through, beat one defender, side-stepped the next, and found that I had come inside him and was positioned to take a pass. I gave the ball back to Macpherson who passed to Hart, took a return pass, drew the Welsh full-back Bassett and sent Simmers racing over at the corner.

I choose this try because it was in the finest tradition of attacking back play and delighted everybody (except the Welsh!).

A. J. (Tony) Ward

(Garryowen, St. Mary's College, Ireland & British Isles)
14 caps for Ireland (1978-84), 1 Test for British Isles (1980) as a stand-off half.
Now lives in Loughlinstown, Co. Dublin.

MOST MEMORABLE PARTICIPATION IN TRY
Munster (12) v New Zealand (0), Limerick, 31.10.1978

Donal Conniffe threw a ball to me going open on the 22. I chanced a chip over the All Black centres and the freak, or lucky, bounce landed in the hands of our left-wing Jimmy Bowen. He went off on a weaving run and when finally checked by the full-back, McKechnie, found Christy Cantillon in support. Our flanker ran the remaining 20 metres for a try at the posts. My conversion and two dropped goals helped to seal the game for Munster.

I choose the try because of the importance of the occasion. It led to a result which is now part of the folklore of Irish Rugby, the first defeat of a New Zealand XV in Ireland.

MOST MEMORABLE TRY WITNESSED
Ireland (14) v Wales (0), Dublin, 14.3.1970

I choose Ken Goodall's famous solo try. I watched it as a 13-year-old schoolboy and it left a lasting impression on me. Also, it was scored against Wales who will always be to Rugby what Brazil are to Association Football, if you know what I mean!

David Watkins

(Newport, Wales & British Isles)
21 caps for Wales (1963-67), 6 Tests for British Isles (1966) as a stand-off half.
Now lives at Newport, Gwent.

MOST MEMORABLE TRY SCORED
Ireland (6) v Wales (15), Dublin, 7.3.1964

The Welsh forwards won a line-out some 40 yards out on our right. On receiving the ball from my scrum-half, Clive Rowlands, I took Mike Gibson, Ireland's stand-off, on the outside and pushed him off before cutting inside Kevin Flynn in the centre. I then had to race outside full-back Keogh and cross just left of the posts.

I choose this try because I was trying to establish myself at international level and needed such a score to boost confidence and belief in myself.

MOST MEMORABLE TRY WITNESSED
Barbarians (3) v New Zealand (36), Cardiff, 15.2.1964

Time was running out as New Zealand skipper Wilson Whineray received the ball some 30 yards out after a combined move and set off for the line. Scottish full-back Stewart Wilson confronted Whineray who, as a prop, was expected to pass to a support player but instead sold an outrageous dummy and went on to cross at the posts for a superb try.

This All Black team was probably one of the best, especially with forwards who included Tremain, Nathan, Stan and Colin Meads, Ken Gray and Whineray himself. Their demolition of the Baa-Baas underlined their capacity for outstanding 15-man Rugby.

M. P. (Mike) Weston

(Richmond, Durham City, England & British Isles)
29 caps for England (1960-68), 6 Tests for British Isles (1962-66) as centre and stand-off half.
Now lives in Durham.

MOST MEMORABLE PARTICIPATION IN TRY
England (3) v Scotland (3), Twickenham, 20.3.1965

With the game in injury time Scotland led by a dropped goal to nil and England were defending within their 25. Receiving the ball from a ruck I went on the blind side and for once, instead of kicking, passed to Andy Hancock. He beat the first line of coverers, picked up speed, kept running, and scored, in the corner to earn England a draw.

Meanwhile I had been late tackled and lost a tooth. Every time I have the false one renewed I am reminded of this try!

MOST MEMORABLE TRY WITNESSED
England (15) v New Zealand (9), Twickenham, 19.11.1983

This was Maurice Colclough's try. He was driven over the line in a concerted move near the All Blacks' line.

I choose this try because it proved that the best way to score against New Zealand is from set-pieces near their line. Furthermore, it enabled England at last to beat New Zealand in a home international match for the first time since 1935.

England show their delight after Colclough has been driven over the All Black line for a vital try in the 1983 match at Twickenham.

Peter Wheeler

(Leicester, England & British Isles)
41 caps for England (1975-84), 7 Tests for the
British Isles (1977-80) as a hooker.
Now lives in Leicester.

MOST MEMORABLE PARTICIPATION IN TRY
Scotland (18) v England (30), Murrayfield, 15.3.1980

It is very difficult to pick out one try from a host of others. For one thing, on television tries look quite different — usually better! — from the way they appeared on the field. However John Carleton's first try (of three) in this game stays in my mind. From a scrummage England number eight John Scott picked up, drew a man and fed the wing who used strength and power to get a touch-down. The foundation of the try was a good scrummage — which gives satisfaction to a hooker.

I like tries which are well orchestrated but also contain a series of reactions to a changing situation.

(below and opposite)
John Carleton outpaces the Scottish defence in England's 1980 triumph at Murrayfield – one of three tries he scored that afternoon.

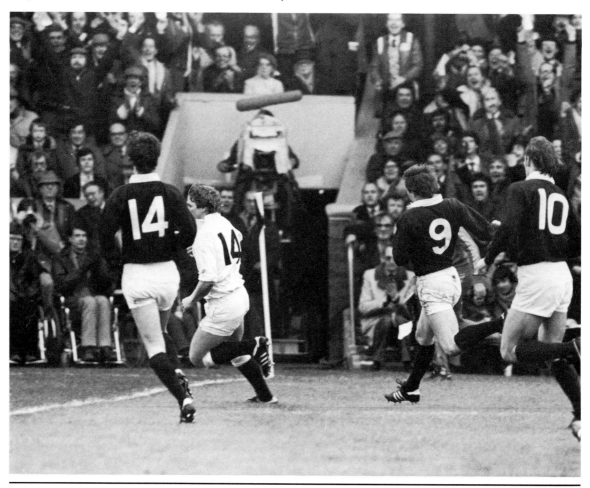

94

Bryan Williams
(Auckland & New Zealand)
38 Tests for New Zealand (1970-78) as a wing.
Now lives in Auckland, New Zealand.

MOST MEMORABLE TRY SCORED
Eastern Province (8) v New Zealand (49), Port Elizabeth, 1.8.1970

Right at the end of the game I failed to latch onto a pass from Bill Davis but the ball bounced off my foot a yard or two upfield beyond the grasp of our opponents. I picked it up about 60 yards from the Eastern Province goal-line and was trying to get into my stride as the cover defence closed in. By a mixture of strength, finesse and good fortune I got through four or five would-be tacklers and found the last 15 yards to the line clear.

I choose this try because it was probably the best I ever scored in terms of beating men by different means — side-step, swerve, fend or hand-off and so on. In the context of the game it was not important, but it lingers in my mind as the favourite.

MOST MEMORABLE TRY WITNESSED
New Zealand (22) v British Isles (12), Christchurch, 10.7.1971

The try scored by Ian Kirkpatrick was magnificent. He broke from a maul near half-way and as four of the Lions' backs confronted him he fended them off like flies. His speed and fend were marvellous to behold!

Bleddyn Williams
(Cardiff, Wales & British Isles)
22 caps for Wales (1947-55), 5 Tests for the British Isles (1950) as a centre and occasional stand-off half.

MOST MEMORABLE TRY SCORED
Wales (3) v South Africa (6), Cardiff, 22.12.1951

As Triple Crown and Grand Slam winners the previous season Wales were expected to give the Springboks the hardest battle in their British Isles Test series. So it proved. South Africa, having applied relentless back-row pressure upon the young Cliff Morgan at stand-off half, led by just a try and a dropped goal with only two minutes left. That was when I worked a scissors move with Malcolm Thomas which sent him clear up to the Springboks' full-back Johnny Buchler. I had stayed close to my fellow centre and was well-placed to take his return pass and score ten yards in from the corner flag.

MOST MEMORABLE PARTICIPATION IN TRY
New Zealand (11) v British Isles (8), Wellington, 1.7.1950

With the British Isles 11-3 down late in the game, I had insisted as skipper that we would run possession from a scrum on our goal-line. So the ball went from Rex Willis (who by this stage was concussed and thought he was playing at Llandaff Fields) via Jackie Kyle and myself to Lewis Jones who broke the defence. Confronted by Bob Scott he fed Ken Jones who went the rest of the way like the Olympic sprinter he was.

In 1983 I went back to New Zealand to follow the Lions' tour of that year. In Hamilton a man came up to me and talked about that very try. Thirty-three years and many Tests later it remained, in his opinion, the best he had ever seen.

J. J. Williams

(Llanelli, Wales & British Isles)
30 caps for Wales (1973-79), 7 Tests for the British
Isles (1974-77) as a wing.
Now lives in Porthcawl, Mid Glamorgan.

MOST MEMORABLE TRY SCORED
South Africa (9) v British Isles (26), Port Elizabeth, 13.7.1974

Collaboration with J. P. R. Williams coming up
from full-back had assisted me to score a first try
with a deft scissors move which left me only a
few yards to cover, and he also helped set up the
second — though this time I was left with much
more to do.

The ball reached me a long way from South
Africa's line and close to touch, where I was
forced by the cover defence to kick ahead. The
ball behaved beautifully, a perfect bounce sitting up into my hands with 20 yards to run. I
was at full speed — and no Springbok was going
to stop me reaching the line.

Our runaway win clinched the series for the
1974 Lions.

MOST MEMORABLE TRY WITNESSED
Barbarians (23) v New Zealand (11), Cardiff, 27.1.1973

The try scored by J. P. R. Williams to end the All
Blacks' fight-back and seal the Baa-Baas' win
was memorable for the number of times the ball
was handled and the duration of play uninter-
rupted by an infringement.

J. J. Williams going full tilt for the line – 'no Springbok was going to stop me.' His try helped the Lions to clinch the 1974 test series.

John Williams

(New South Wales & Australia)
3 Tests for Australia (1963) as a wing.
Now lives in Sydney, Australia.

MOST MEMORABLE TRIES SCORED
South Africa (9) v Australia (11), Johannesburg, 24.8.1963

This try, the only one of the match, came 25 minutes into the second half and was scored at great speed, probably in less than 15 seconds.

It started at a line-out near half-way, where Rob Heming made a magnificent jump at number seven and deflected the ball to Peter Crittle who had peeled off, French style. He made considerable distance towards my wing before turning his back on the Springbok defenders who had no idea what was coming next. Outside centre Dick Marks it was who took a short pass and ran hard at my opposite number Gert Cilliers.

I had not taken my eye off the ball since Heming's deflection, and now received from Dick Marks one of the most perfect passes I ever had. I ran onto it, took it at arm's length and, through sheer pace and closeness to the ground, reached the flag untouched.

My career was cut short by injury, but of the many tries I scored this lasts longest in my memory. I'm sure the 70,000 spectators will remember it, even if only because it sealed victory for Australia in the Third Test of the 1963 series — the first time the Wallabies beat the Springboks in two straight Tests since 1896.

Eastern Transvaal (0) v Australia (14), Spring, 15.6.1963

In this opening game of the 1963 tour the altitude — 6,000 feet above sea level — made it hard for the Wallabies, but I guess the team was acclimatizing itself during the game as all our points came in the second half, including a try by me on my debut for Australia.

The forwards won loose possession which was initially somewhat slow, but then Peter Jones took up the running and made a fine break. As I received the ball I was at top speed and won the race to the corner. The try made me feel much better, for I had dropped a scoring pass in the first half.

J. P. R. Williams

(Bridgend, London Welsh, Wales & British Isles).
55 caps for Wales (1969-81), 8 Tests for British
Isles (1971-74) as a full-back.
Now lives near Cowbridge, South Glamorgan.

MOST MEMORABLE TRY SCORED
Barbarians (23) v New Zealand (11), Cardiff, 27.1.1973

After trailing 17-0 at half-time the All Blacks
had fought back to within six points of the
Baa-Baas. My try, however, put us back in the
driving seat and made sure of victory. The ball
was in play for some 90 seconds, at the end of
which I received a pass from Fergus Slattery
and beat the opposition full-back Joe Karam
with a laboured side-step.

After the ball had remained in play for so
long, to round off the move with a vital try was a
great thrill for me. I don't think I was ever as
tired in the whole of my playing career, and
trying to run back to the half-way line was a
considerable effort!

MOST MEMORABLE PARTICIPATION IN TRY
Scotland (9) v Wales (18), Murrayfield, 19.3.1977

The decisive try for Wales. It was started in our
own 22 when I fell on the ball and transferred to
Steve Fenwick. He set up a counter-attack
carried on by Gerald Davies and David Burcher
which ended up with a try by Phil Bennett.

I choose it for one reason — that it highlights
a successful attack out of a defensive position
which was very tight.

The other side of the coin. Grant Batty, the All Blacks winger, is disgusted after failing to prevent J. P. R. Williams's try for the Barbarians in 1973.

Les Williams
(Llanelli, Cardiff & Wales)
7 caps for Wales (1947-49) as a wing.
Now lives in Penryn, Cornwall.

MOST MEMORABLE TRY SCORED
Wales (9) v England (3), Cardiff, 15.1.1949

Five minutes from the end of the game with Wales 6-3 up Glyn Davies received from Tanner and produced a brilliant piece of stand-off half play, beating three defenders before drawing the England full-back and passing to me for a clear 25-yard sprint to the corner.

I choose this try because it was the culmination of great half-back play — resulting in what every wing hopes for: to be given the ball with no one to beat. It was my second try of the match, and made the game safe for Wales. It was also my last try as a Rugby Union player.

MOST MEMORABLE TRY WITNESSED
Scotland (9) v Wales (18), Murrayfield, 19.3.1977

This try began in the Welsh 25 and finished with Phil Bennett scoring between the Scottish posts. I choose it because it had attack from defence, man beating man, good backing up, and accurate passing under pressure. A classic length-of-field try.

(below and opposite)
Phil Bennett shows his extraordinary ability to leave would-be tacklers floundering on his way to one of the great tries of modern Rugby – against the Scots at Murrayfield in 1977.

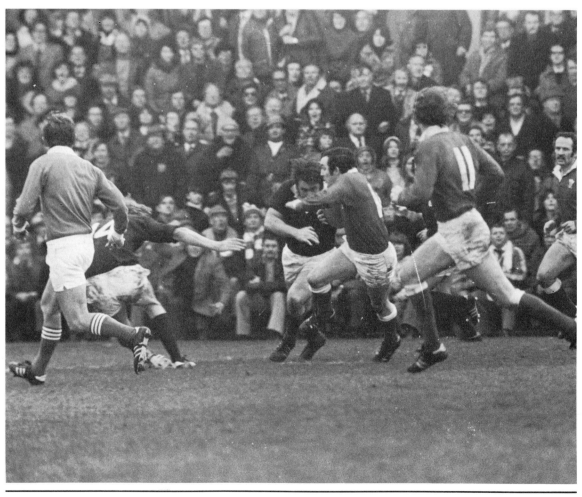

R. H. (Rhys) Williams
(Llanelli, Wales & British Isles)
23 caps for Wales (1954-60), 10 Tests for British Isles (1955-59) as a lock-forward.
Now lives in Cardiff, South Glamorgan.

S. S. (Stu) Wilson
(Wellington & New Zealand)
27 Tests for New Zealand (1977-83) as a wing.
Now lives at Wellington, New Zealand.

MOST MEMORABLE PARTICIPATION IN TRY
South Africa (22) v British Isles (23), Johannesburg, 6.8.1955

A Cliff Morgan try. Following a strike against the head on South Africa's 25-line and a sharp delivery from Dickie Jeeps, Cliff feinted to come inside only to veer on a wide arc outside Basie van Wyk, the flanker to score.

The try and the occasion are memorable for many reasons. A record 95,000 crowd saw the game. The Lions bravely overcame the loss of flanker Reg Higgins. It was a great personal joy to be on the right side of the scrummage behind Courtenay Meredith and Bryn Meredith to win the strike. And Cliff's effort was a case of sweet revenge, since as a youngster he had been outwitted by van Wyk when South Africa beat Wales in 1951.

MOST MEMORABLE TRIES WITNESSED

All short-range tries by Gareth Edwards!

More often that not such tries by him were almost predictable to all — players and spectators alike. But they were all outstanding tries because:
a great team effort had already been produced to arrive at the position for a final assault;
the part played by the pack in gaining good possession was paramount for Gareth to be able to strike;
Gareth's final strength and skill in getting across the line were tremendous.

MOST MEMORABLE TRY SCORED
New Zealand (40) v Scotland (15), Auckland, 20.6.1981

Ten minutes into the game — New Zealand pressurizing Scotland within their 22. From a line-out the All Black forwards won the ball, for Dave Loveridge to send his backline away towards the All Black right and my wing. Our first five-eighth missed out the inside-centre and Bernie Fraser came in from the left wing alongside the outside-centre to draw a defender and put me clear. I had seen the Scots madly covering towards the corner and decided to take a very straight course to the line hoping to catch them wrong-footed.

If the truth be known I did not have the speed to outflank the defenders and somehow, instinctively, Bernie sensed my angle and gave me a lovely short pass off his right shoulder on the burst. With my angle and speed I went in between the Scottish outside-centre, who had drifted onto Bernie, and Bruce Hay my opposite number. With the same straight angle I cut further inside Andy Irvine and then saw only Roy Laidlaw to beat. He was too far over in cover, and I went inside him to score behind Scotland's posts.

What can be learned from a try like that? Mainly, that defenders must go across the field in waves. In this case all the Scots were rushing across in cover together thinking they would bundle me out at the corner; this was tactically sound — but what about someone cutting back against the tide and running straight for the goal-line? As it was, no-one was in a good position to make an effective tackle on me.

I choose this try because it is very difficult to score tries from set-pieces. Usually in New Zealand they result from second, third or fourth-phase possession.

Stu Wilson in full flight for the All Blacks. He scored a marvellous try from a set-piece against Scotland in 1981.

MOST MEMORABLE TRY WITNESSED
New Zealand (22) v British Isles (12), Christchurch, 10.7.1971

Ian Kirkpatrick ran the full length of the field for his try using all his strength to maintain top speed on the heavy ground. He just kept running with the ball in one hand. Even the famous JPR missed him in the tackle.

That was a sight to remember. The try typified everything about 'Kirky': fast, powerful, competitive — all the qualities New Zealand fans look for in a loose forward. To see him run such a distance fending off defenders at will was a sight to see.

Bobby Windsor

(Pontypool, Wales & British Isles)
28 caps for Wales (1973-79), 5 Tests for British
Isles (1974-77) as a hooker.
Now lives in Newport, Gwent.

MOST MEMORABLE TRY SCORED
Wales (24) v Australia (0), Cardiff, 10.11.1973

This was Wales's first win over a touring side for
fifteen years, and I was winning a first cap. My
try, in injury time, was the third by Wales and it
cannot have been very spectacular as I have
never seen it shown on television. However, to
me it was a 50-yard one!

MOST MEMORABLE PARTICIPATION IN TRY
France (10) v Wales (25), Paris, 18.1.1975

Nobody had given Wales a chance before the
kick-off. However we had a new-look side with
nothing to lose, and among our six new caps was
Graham Price who joined me and Tony Faulkner to make this the first time the Pontypool
front row appeared together in a full international game.

Pricey's try, Wales's fifth, in injury time at the
end of the game, made his representative debut
unforgettable. A French attack broke down on
the Welsh 22, and he found the energy to chase
a fly-hack 75 yards, gather the ball and charge
the last few paces for a thrilling try.

*Bobby Windsor on the charge for Wales. He scored a try on his
international debut against Australia in 1973.*

Wilfred Wooller

(Sale, Cambridge University, Cardiff & Wales)
18 caps for Wales (1933-39) as centre and wing.
Now lives in Cardiff.

MOST MEMORABLE PARTICIPATION IN TRY
Wales (13) v New Zealand (12), Cardiff, 21.12.1935

This game is still rated the most exciting and fluctuating contest ever staged at Cardiff. Wales led 10-3 at half-time. New Zealand fought back to go ahead 12-10 with ten minutes remaining. A scrummage collapsed; the Welsh hooker Don Tarr was side-lined with a broken neck; a key man gone, fourteen men were left to fight on; the crowd was silenced in gloom

Then our seven forwards rose to the occasion magnificently and the tight-packed crowd woke up. The adrenalin flowed. We were uplifted. It was a superb example of massed will at work — almost uncanny.

Wales heeled from a set scrummage on the half-way line towards the South Stand. Haydn Tanner's swift pass was reached, with his finger tips, by Cliff Jones who shot off like a jet. I was at top speed when I got his pass — and Claude Davey was cutting towards me for an inside break when I realized that Oliver, who was marking him, had been drawn in too. I checked, ran round Claude and inside the New Zealand wing Ball and was away in the open towards the Taff end. I sensed a covering wing-forward; All Black full-back Gilbert moved into my path; no sign of my right-wing, Geoffrey Rees Jones. I tapped the ball over Gilbert's head, not high — 20 feet, maybe — a much-practised short kick. I ran onto the dropping ball with the goal-line a few yards distant. No one in my way. I must score.

The ball hit ground that was hard from overnight frost and rose perpendicularly. I grabbed at it, but it was too high and I missed it, shooting on into the thick straw behind the dead-ball line. It was as I hit it that I heard the crowd roar, hysterically loudly. I did not know what had happened, but as I looked back to the corner I saw Rees Jones, ball and all, lying over the goal-line. The crowd were in an uproar, the noise deafening. Hats, which were worn in those days, sailed up into the air. Arms were raised. With three minutes to go Wales had scored and won an historic victory.

When I put together the final seconds, I learned that the ball had eluded not only me but also the turning All Black full-back Gilbert. Rees Jones, coming up behind, had caught it to score wide out.

MOST MEMORABLE TRY WITNESSED
Ireland (3) v Wales (6), Belfast, 11.3.1950

Ireland alone stood between Wales, who had beaten England 11-5 and Scotland 12-0, and a first Triple Crown for 39 years. Minutes remained, with the score tied at 3-3. Then at a scrummage Ray Cale pounced upon the Irish halves Carroll and Kyle and the ball went loose.

Welsh stand-off Billy Cleaver picked up and fed Lewis Jones in the centre. He broke left, drew full-back Norton, and sent a long pass to Malcolm Thomas who was 15 yards out. The wing put his head back and ran for the corner, diving through a flurry of frantic defenders. The corner flag went down.

An agonizing lifetime of seconds went by. Then Irish touch-judge Ossie Glasgow indicated a fair touch down and referee R. A. Beattie raised his arm — Wales had won! A magnificent climax to a battle of giants — and the first Triple Crown victory in my lifetime.

Peter Yarranton

(RAF, Wasps & England)
5 caps for England (1954-55) as a lock-forward.
Now lives in Teddington, Middlesex.

MOST MEMORABLE PARTICIPATION IN TRY
England (9) v Wales (6), Twickenham, 16.1.1954

This game brought me a first cap. I had prayed for a dream debut against the Welsh — and by and large was having one. At half-time it was 3-3, with tries by Gwyn Rowlands for the opposition and Ted Woodward for us.

Woodward scored again to put us ahead and my world was complete until, right in front of the committee and selection box, I was penalized for barging. It seemed a no-risk penalty as Rowlands (an RAF colleague) teed it up — out on the touch-line and at half-way. To my horror his kick sailed between the posts. I could feel hostility everywhere and resigned myself to becoming a one-cap wonder.

Then, with no time left and Wales pounding our line, Pat Quinn picked up a loose ball and began running upfield. Baulked at the half-way line he found Martin Regan outside him. Then Tug Wilson took over at about 30 yards' range going left. He was quickly grounded, but John MacG. Kendall-Carpenter steamed up from nowhere to keep the attack going, only to be corner-flagged about five yards short. Four of us piled into the loose scrum. I heeled the ball back to John MacG. He found wing Chris Winn, who dived over.

Deep down, I knew they would never drop a new boy, penalty and all, after a first-of-the-season win over Wales!

MOST MEMORABLE TRY WITNESSED
England (10) v Scotland (8), Twickenham, 16.3.1963

Richard Sharp's captaincy of England brought far more than an unbeaten record and some fine tries. He deserved, like Barry John later, good quick ball — and to forwards his presence was magic: you really wanted to get the ball to him because you knew he would do something with it.

In this end-of season Championship decider Scotland were ahead 8-5 at half-time and England did not look as though they could do much about it. From a scrum just inside Scotland's half on the England left Simon Clarke zoomed a long pass to Sharp who dummied a pass to Mike Weston causing the Scottish back row to shoot past. After hesitating just enough to check full-back Blaikie, he set off like a hare to score without a finger being laid on him. Wilcox's conversion sealed England's win.

Dennis Young

(Canterbury & New Zealand)

22 Tests for New Zealand (1956-64) as a hooker.
Now lives in Christchurch, New Zealand.

MOST MEMORABLE PARTICIPATION IN TRY
Barbarians (3) v New Zealand (36), Cardiff, 15.2.1964

The 1963-64 All Blacks were very successful, but doubts had been expressed about their ability to play the 15-man game. This match provided the answer to critics, and thrilled a capacity crowd. Any one of the seven tries we had scored as the final moments arrived could have been regarded as a classic — but the best was still to come.

The skipper, Wilson Whineray, had achieved many things on tour including the respect of the British Press and Rugby public — but had not been able to score a try. Now, at last, a break having been made by Little and Graham, the supporting Whineray received the ball and set his sights on the goal-line. There was one man to beat before he could score and, although support was available, I doubt if passing the ball ever occurred to Wilson.

Side-stepping props are not unique at representative level but they are to say the least rare. The All Black captain produced a side-step that day at Cardiff Arms Park which would have gladdened the heart of the best of backs. He stormed in for his try — and the crowd went wild. As the game ended they sang 'For he's a jolly good fellow' in an indescribable atmosphere brought about not only by the quality of the try but also out of respect for the scorer and the timing.

I choose the try because, as the last scored by New Zealand on that tour to Britain and France, it provided a perfect finale. A fictional climax could not have been scripted more aptly.

End-piece
By David Parry-Jones

In the years after the Second War many fifteen-year-olds in Cardiff who were apprehensive about impending mathematics examinations for the School Certificate went to be coached by an old gentleman with a warm, wide smile who lived on Penylan Hill. Any pupil wishing to introduce some light relief into the cramming period, so it was said, had only to ask: 'But did Deans really score?' Whereupon the eyes of their tutor would turn dim and distant while his imagination scanned an action-replay from four decades earlier; and then he would smile and say, 'No. I tackled him short of the line. He tried to wriggle over. The referee ruled against him.'

For this was Rhys Gabe — not only a member of the 1905 Welsh XV at Cardiff which robbed the First All Blacks of an unbeaten tour record, but also the man who prevented Bob Deans scoring late in the game to cancel out Teddy Morgan's precious try for Wales in the first half. Though the post-match banquet passed without incident, on the following Monday morning the *Daily Mail* newspaper published a claim by Deans that he had touched down over the Welsh line only to be pulled back by defenders before the arrival of the referee. Forty years on small boys anxiously sought first-hand comment on the genial controversy thus engendered; eighty years later it still ticks over.

Through the recall of active participants this book has celebrated the scoring and witnessing of outstanding tries. The mood of the contributions is macho, their dominant emotion exultancy — and with justification. For, turning the theme on its head, nothing is more shattering or destructive of morale — both to players and their supporters — than being on the receiving end of a great try. Conceding a dropped goal or penalty is something that can be shrugged off. A try paralyses — literally, since the unsuccessful defenders must line up helplessly while an opponent kicks at their goal for bonus points. A try is the ball that knocks the off-stump clean out of the ground. A try is a punch to the point of the jaw. A try is, in short, an incontrovertible statement about relative merit. That is why the Welsh never tired of hearing from the lips of Rhys Gabe and his contemporaries the four magic words, 'Deans did not score.'

But there were others who did. And just as, doubtless, a try by Gareth Edwards or Gerald Davies was felt by the opposing camp as a rapier-thrust below the ribs, so there have been men whose tries against Welsh defences seemed terminal to onlooking partisans. Such player was Jim Kearney whose Boxing Day try for the Kiwis in 1945 extended the tourists' unbeaten run to twelve matches and inflicted a first defeat of the season upon a star-studded Cardiff XV. Proctor, Kearney, Allen, Smith, Argus and finally Kearney again were involved, and though the score came after only ten minutes I vividly recall the feeling that any team able to produce such a move was unlikely to lose the game. So it proved.

That feeling came again on 20 October 1951. Again Cardiff were the victims but this time the invaders were the Fourth Springboks, also an unbeaten side at this juncture of their tour. With only minutes left they were behind 9-8 but pressurizing the Welsh team on its 10-metre line. At a scrummage the Springbok forwards produced good ball for stand-off half Hannes Brewis to float a superb diagonal kick towards the corner flag. Away to his left 'Chum' Ochse sniffed the wind and, brushing his way past defender Alun Thomas, set off in pursuit as a dutiful wing. At the same time Cardiff full-back Frank Trott began his corner-flagging run, reacting to the danger a fatal quarter of a second late. Through every despairing stride all fifty thousand of us willed the defender's weary leg muscles to edge his frame ahead of the speeding Springbok: to no avail. Gently the ball rolled over the goal-line; passionately Ochse reached it first. The blow was struck, and presumed no recovery.

In Press boxes, or when microphones are being employed, hearts are worn beneath sleeves. Notwithstanding, if one is Welsh — or English or Scottish or whatever — that sunken feeling, that certainty that all is indeed lost, can still arrive. I knew it when Graham Mourie scored the opening try for New Zealand against Wales in 1980 — described elsewhere so graphically by him; and I knew it again at Twickenham in 1982.

This was a day when, despite scores by Slemen and Hare, onlookers were pushed to work out why the lead lay with England. Though still pointless half an hour into the game the Welsh were competing hard. Their backs seemed full of running, their pack still breathed fire through forwards like Clive Burgess. After an aggressive counter-attack by his side the Ebbw Vale flanker took out England scrum half Steve Smith to set up a ruck near the Welsh 10-metre line on the East Stand side. Here it was that, espying his chance, right wing John Carleton nipped in to seize the loose ball and accelerate away towards the 22 past forwards who still had their heads down, leaving the surprised Terry Holmes and Clive Rees in his wake. An outside swerve wrong-footed Gwyn Evans and

110

the man from Orrell went to the goal-line still travelling like a rocket. Welsh heads drooped, for good; a glum, inescapable awareness of shortcomings pervaded the red presence on field and terraces. Once again a try had been a clinical, devastating, and ultimately murderous thrust.

An ever-increasing volume of concern has been expressed recently about the part penalties play at the expense of tries in deciding modern Rugby matches. People are right to agitate, and makers of the Laws must always make sure that punishments fit crimes without stifling free enterprise. But the glory and pre-eminence of tries as the preferred method of winning will never be undermined.

With respect to Don Clark, Okey Geffin, Keith Jarrett, Bob Hiller, Dusty Hare, Tom Kiernan, Pierre Villepreux, Andy Irvine and the other great place-kickers it is not possible to imagine a book about memorable penalty goals.

And if there were one, you would not buy it.

(following pages)
Whether it was the best try ever is much disputed, but it must be the best-known. This sequence, taken from the BBC video film, shows the full movement which led to Gareth Edwards's breathtaking try for the Barbarians against the All Blacks in 1973. It started deep in the Barbarians' 25, where Phil Bennett jinked his way out of trouble to launch the move. A brilliant tapestry of passing and running followed, before Edwards showed electrifying pace and power to score the try which is now part of Rugby folklore.